YOUTH OR EXPERIENCE?

MARTIN BINKIN *and* IRENE KYRIAKOPOULOS

YOUTH OR EXPERIENCE?

Manning the Modern Military

THE BROOKINGS INSTITUTION

Washington, D.C.

Library of Congress Cataloging in Publication Data:

Binkin, Martin, 1928–
  Youth or experience?

  (Studies in defense policy; 21)
  Includes bibliographical references.
    1. Manpower policy—United States.   2. United States
—Armed Forces.   I. Kyriakopoulos, Irene, joint author.
II. Title.   III. Series.
UA17.5.U5B56   355.2′2   79-12633
ISBN 0-8157-0969-2

9 8 7 6 5 4 3 2 1

THE BROOKINGS INSTITUTION is an independent organization devoted to nonpartisan research, education, and publication in economics, government, foreign policy, and the social sciences generally. Its principal purposes are to aid in the development of sound public policies and to promote public understanding of issues of national importance.

The Institution was founded on December 8, 1927, to merge the activities of the Institute for Government Research, founded in 1916, the Institute of Economics, founded in 1922, and the Robert Brookings Graduate School of Economics and Government, founded in 1924.

The Board of Trustees is responsible for the general administration of the Institution, while the immediate direction of the policies, program, and staff is vested in the President, assisted by an advisory committee of the officers and staff. The by-laws of the Institution state: "It is the function of the Trustees to make possible the conduct of scientific research, and publication, under the most favorable conditions, and to safeguard the independence of the research staff in the pursuit of their studies and in the publication of the results of such studies. It is not a part of their function to determine, control, or influence the conduct of particular investigations or the conclusions reached."

The President bears final responsibility for the decision to publish a manuscript as a Brookings book. In reaching his judgment on the competence, accuracy, and objectivity of each study, the President is advised by the director of the appropriate research program and weighs the views of a panel of expert outside readers who report to him in confidence on the quality of the work. Publication of a work signifies that it is deemed a competent treatment worthy of public consideration but does not imply endorsement of conclusions or recommendations.

The Institution maintains its position of neutrality on issues of public policy in order to safeguard the intellectual freedom of the staff. Hence interpretations or conclusions in Brookings publications should be understood to be solely those of the authors and should not be attributed to the Institution, to its trustees, officers, or other staff members, or to the organizations that support its research.

108279

FOREWORD

DURING much of its history the U.S. military establishment has managed its human resources within the confines of a unique system largely unaffected by the rules of the American marketplace. This arrangement was taken for granted in pre-World War II days when small peacetime U.S. forces of mostly unskilled personnel were backed up by wartime conscription, and it continued to escape serious question even when the nation adopted a large postwar standing army supported by peacetime conscription. In recent years, however, several converging trends have focused attention on some of the problems associated with the status quo.

First, the cost of military manpower has increased sharply over the past decade as a result of lessening the differences between military and civilian pay and of underwriting the all-volunteer armed forces. With the end of conscription in 1973, the element of the "free good" in military manpower was virtually eliminated.

Second, advances in technology have transformed the occupational needs of the armed forces. Unlike earlier eras when the services consisted mainly of combat personnel engaged in purely military duties, today the armed forces include large numbers of specialists and technicians responsible for tasks similar to those performed by workers in the private sector.

Finally, as a consequence of demographic patterns, the "aging" of America will soon have far-reaching implications for the armed forces. A sharp decline in the number of youths entering the labor force will make recruitment particularly difficult.

This study of the military's extensive reliance on youth is a first step in the important task of reconsidering whether current military manpower policies, many strongly anchored in tradition, are appropriate today in the face of economic, technological, and demographic change. After examining the age profile of the armed forces and the factors that shape it, the authors contend that policies yielding a young and necessarily inexperienced military force should not be sustained. They argue that the retention of trained workers for longer terms of service would improve the match between the occupational requirements of the modern military and its work force. They conclude that policies fostering a more experienced military establishment would enable the nation to field more effective forces—and perhaps save money as well.

The authors' purpose is not to prescribe an optimal age and experience composition for the military work force. Rather, they explain why they believe that the policies now governing the manning of the armed forces should be changed, assess the cost of making such a change, and identify those aspects of the military personnel system that require alteration if the nation is to obtain the maximum return on its investment in defense manpower.

Martin Binkin and Irene Kyriakopoulos are members of the research staff of the Brookings Foreign Policy Studies program, which is under the direction of John D. Steinbruner. Their study is the twenty-first in the Brookings Studies in Defense Policy series. They are grateful to Philip A. Odeen and General Bruce Palmer, Jr., for helpful comments during the preparation of the manuscript, as well as to Michael W. Bryant, Robert F. Hale, Gary R. Nelson, Bernard D. Rostker, G. Thomas Sicilia, Neil M. Singer, and George F. Travers. They are indebted further to numerous officials in the Office of the Secretary of Defense; the staff of the Assistant Secretary of Defense for Manpower, Reserve Affairs, and Logistics; and the Defense Manpower Data Center for data and assistance.

The authors also thank their Brookings colleagues John D. Steinbruner and John L. Palmer for valuable suggestions, Tadd Fisher for editing the manuscript, Ellen W. Smith for verifying its factual content, and Ann M. Ziegler for bearing the secretarial burden.

The Institution acknowledges the assistance of the Ford Foundation and the Rockefeller Foundation, whose grants helped to support this study. The views expressed here are those of the authors and should not be ascribed to the persons who provided data or who commented on the manuscript, to the Ford or Rockefeller Foundations, or to the trustees, officers, or other staff members of the Brookings Institution.

BRUCE K. MACLAURY
President

March 1979
Washington, D.C.

CONTENTS

Tables

INTRODUCTION

IN RECENT YEARS the effectiveness of the U.S. military forces has become a subject of considerable interest, widespread debate, and some worry. Much of this concern has centered on the issue of whether the volunteers now manning the armed forces are up to the task of protecting vital U.S. national security interests. Indeed, whether the nation should even attempt to maintain a large standing military establishment by voluntary means has come under question.

Some critics lament supposed deterioration in the quality of the volunteer forces, others deplore the drain imposed on the defense budget by the growing military payroll, and some worry that shortages in the reserve forces are compromising the nation's mobilization capabilities. There are also ideological concerns: some observers are disturbed because a larger proportion of blacks are now in the armed forces than are in the general population, and others fear that the American military system has been changed from a "calling" with special institutional values into just another occupation that emphasizes monetary rewards.

For the most part these issues have been joined within the context of prevailing manpower policies and practices, some of which may no longer be appropriate. One such practice, originally tailored to fit the needs of a military establishment of an earlier era, is the armed forces' heavy reliance on youth. Maintaining a work force in which more than half of the members are under the age of 24 has particularly important implications for the problems at hand.

A youthful force generates a relatively high turnover of personnel (on the average the military reconstitutes itself every five years), thus giving rise to a large demand for new recruits (upwards of 400,000 a year). As long as the nation relied on conscripted manpower, military pay was inordinately low, particularly in the lower grades; hence turnover was cheap. But since the end of the draft, as disproportionate increases in pay and benefits have been accorded junior enlisted personnel and as the cost of recruiting and sustaining volunteers has grown substantially, turnover has imposed a large and growing burden on the defense budget.

Moreover, a young force is an inexperienced force. As long as the armed services principally needed physically robust but relatively un-skilled people, the experience factor was secondary. But the military services have kept pace with major technological developments, pioneer-ing them in some instances, and in so doing have created a greater need for technical know-how. Thus the appropriateness of a military work force in which close to 40 percent of the employees are apprentices, helpers, or trainees is called into question.

Which military manpower procurement and utilization policies yield this young and inexperienced force? How appropriate are such policies in light of technological, economic, and demographic trends? What are the cost and effectiveness implications of changes in the policies? These are among the questions addressed in this study. Its purpose is not to prescribe the optimal age and experience composition of the armed forces, but rather to explore and explain why any change is necessary, to illustrate the cost-effectiveness of change in the experience composition, and to identify the shortcomings of the military personnel system that now cir-cumscribe the potential for instituting more than modest improvements in the experience mix.

The study begins with an examination of the factors that shape the age and experience mix in the military forces and a brief review of the evolu-tion of the armed forces' occupational structure. Then, an assessment of the match-up between the current roster of military jobs and the age and experience of persons now manning those positions indicates the potential benefits of enhancing the experience composition of the armed forces. This is followed by a discussion of the implications for the reserve forces and for society of changes in the experience mix of the active forces. Next, budgetary considerations are taken into account. What are the relative costs of holding on to experienced workers, on the one hand, or of replac-ing them with inexperienced recruits, on the other? This trade-off is quan-tified and its implications are discussed.

The study concludes with proposals for moving toward a more ap-propriate experience mix in the armed forces. The possibilities of achiev-ing more experienced armed forces within the present policy framework are explored, as well as more far-reaching modifications that would call for fundamental changes in the way the military compensates its personnel and for substantial changes in legislation.

For simplicity, the analysis is confined to the armed forces' enlisted component, which constitutes close to 90 percent of total military manpower. The principles employed in this study, however, could also be applied generally to the officer corps.

CHAPTER TWO

ACCENT ON YOUTH

THE ARMED FORCES are the nation's largest single employer of youth. In fiscal year 1979 the military will "hire" about 350,000 new recruits, and if past experience is a guide, most will still be in their teens. This number represents a slight decrease from the average over the past few years; from fiscal year 1974 through fiscal 1978 an average of about 384,000 young men and women volunteered for military service annually.

This yearly influx of youth is tacitly encouraged by the military establishment, which has always emphasized the importance of a young force. Of some 1.8 million enlisted personnel on the rolls in 1977, 60 percent were under 25 years of age and close to 90 percent were under 35. This reliance on the younger members of the labor force is made clearer in table 2-1, which compares the age distribution of the enlisted inventory with that of employed workers in the civilian sector.[1] The contrast is striking; only 8 percent of civilian workers are younger than 20 years of age and less than one-quarter are under 25. And viewed from another angle, 33 percent of the civilian labor force is over 44 years of age, while only a negligible 1 percent of enlisted personnel is in that age category.

As table 2-2 shows, the armed forces' disproportionate dependence on young people is not of recent origin. At least as far back as 1920 the emphasis on youth is visible, and the median age has remained relatively unchanged since then.[2] And it is unlikely, given the present course, that

1. This study focuses on civilian males in comparisons of data for the civilian and military enlisted work forces, since the enlisted force is predominantly male (94 percent in 1977). As table 2-1 shows, however, the analysis is little affected when extended to the total civilian work force, which includes females.

2. The differences that are evident are more likely to have derived from adjustments in inventory caused by previous expansions and contractions in the size of the military establishment than from changes in underlying policies. For example, the relatively large number of older personnel in 1930 was largely the result of the

Table 2-1. Age Distribution of Military Enlisted Personnel and Civilian Sector Employed Workers, 1977
Percent

	Age				
Category	Under 20	20–24	25–34	35–44	Over 44
Military enlisted personnel	18	42	27	11	1
Civilian sector employed workers	8	14	26	19	33
Male workers	8	13	26	19	34

Sources: Data for military personnel were provided by the Office of the Assistant Secretary of Defense for Manpower, Reserve Affairs, and Logistics. Data for civilian workers are from *Employment and Training Report of the President, 1978* (Government Printing Office, 1978), table A-14, p. 202. Percentages are rounded.

Table 2-2. Age Distribution of Male Military Personnel on Active Duty, Selected Years[a]
Percent

	Male military personnel on active duty						
Age	1920	1930	1940[b]	1950	1960	1970	1976
Under 20	23.4	13.3	19.0	19.1	17.0	13.6	16.8
20–24	37.3	36.8	40.9	36.2	36.7	49.7	37.0
Over 24	39.3	49.9	40.1	44.7	46.3	36.7	46.2
Median age	23	24	24	24	24	23	24

Sources: Data for 1920–40 are from U.S. Bureau of the Census, *Fourteenth Census of the United States Taken in the Year 1920*, vol. 4: *Population 1920, Occupations* (GPO, 1923), table 6, pp. 392–93; *Fifteenth Census of the United States: 1930, Population*, vol. 5: *General Report on Occupations* (GPO, 1933), table 6, pp. 132–33; and *Sixteenth Census of the United States: 1940, Population*, vol. 3: *The Labor Force: Occupation, Industry, Employment, and Income* (GPO, 1943), pt. 1: *United States Summary*, table 65, p. 99. Data for 1950–60 are from U.S. Department of Defense, Office of the Assistant Secretary, Comptroller, *Selected Manpower Statistics, 1973* (DOD, 1973), p. 39; and ibid., *1977* (DOD, 1977), table 311B, pp. 42–43.
a. Data, except for 1940, include both officers and enlisted personnel and are not directly comparable to the data in table 2-1, which pertains to enlisted personnel only.
b. Excludes commissioned officers, professional and clerical workers, and craftsmen.

the overall age composition of the armed forces will change much in the future. Although age is not an explicit planning variable, the services do have long-term objectives for attaining a desired distribution of "first-term" and "career" components of the enlisted force. The Pentagon defines the former as including those personnel who have served less than four years. Table 2-3 shows that the proportion in that group varies among and within the services across time. If their long-range objectives come to pass, the Army and the Navy will move toward more mature forces, the Marine Corps will remain about the same, and the average age of Air

World War I "hump"—the cluster of people who had entered the service during the war years and remained for a full career. By the same token, the decline in the percentage of younger military personnel in 1970 reflects the diminishing need for new recruits as the nation began to reduce its involvement in Southeast Asia.

Table 2-3. Military Enlisted Personnel with Less than Four Years of Service, by Service, Selected Fiscal Years

	Percent of enlisted personnel serving less than four years			
Service	1965	1973	1977	Long-range objective, as of October 1978
Army	66	66	63	59
Navy	61	60	58	55
Marine Corps	66	73	74	74
Air Force	44	50	46	57
Department of Defense total	58	60	59	59

Source: Data for 1965 and 1973 are from U.S. Department of Defense, *Manpower Requirements Report for FY 1975* (DOD, 1974), p. XV-13; 1977 data and long-range objectives are based on unpublished data provided by the Office of the Assistant Secretary of Defense for Manpower, Reserve Affairs, and Logistics.

Force personnel will decline considerably, thus marking a shift toward a less experienced force—perhaps the youngest in Air Force history.

Factors Accounting for the Military's Age Profile

What constitutes the basis for the military's heavy reliance on the nation's youth? Several factors are involved. First, the military has traditionally set a premium on "youth and vigor," largely on the grounds that military occupations demand high levels of physical fitness. Second, the military personnel management system, geared to a traditional pyramidal rank structure, has shaped a force characterized by a high rate of turnover; this has created a requirement for large numbers of young people, who by and large are not expected to serve beyond one enlistment period. Third, a youthful force has long been considered a less expensive force. Fourth, the practice of cycling many of the nation's youth through the active military forces enlarges the mobilization base by providing a source of manpower for U.S. reserve components. Finally, a military system in which a large number of youngsters serve temporarily has also been measured in terms of its benefits for society.

"Youth and Vigor" in the Armed Forces

The military's disproportionate dependence on the younger members of the nation's population has been justified in part on the grounds that military tasks—particularly those relating to combat—demand a level of

Table 2-4. Age Distribution of Military Enlisted Personnel, by Service, June 1977
Percent

Service	*Under 20*	*20–24*	*25–34*	*35–44*	*Over 44*
			Age		
Army	20	42	26	9	1
Navy	19	42	27	11	1
Marine Corps	29	49	16	5	*
Air Force	11	39	32	15	1
Department of Defense total	18	42	27	11	1

Source: Unpublished data provided by the Office of the Assistant Secretary of Defense for Manpower, Reserve Affairs, and Logistics. Percentages are rounded.
* Less than 0.5 percent.

physical prowess most often associated with youthfulness. The perceived synonymity of combat and arduous physical activity stems from popularized images, such as that of the World War II infantryman, equipment-laden and slogging long distances through the jungles of Guadalcanal.

As the stereotype would suggest, the Army and especially the Marine Corps—both of which continue to use combat infantrymen—have a high proportion of enlisted members aged 17 to 24. Table 2-4 shows that 62 percent of Army and almost 80 percent of Marine Corps enlisted personnel are less than 25 years old, while the corresponding figures for the Navy and the Air Force are 61 percent and 50 percent, respectively.

But the youth-and-vigor concept has been extended beyond the combat soldier. Since personnel assigned to noncombat duties in peacetime are viewed as an emergency pool of combat replacements in wartime, the services contend that everyone should be physically fit: at a minimum all enlistees must be "combat fit" with "no significant assignment limitations."[3] This standard reflects the belief that the more combat fit the force is, the more effective it is. Thus the younger the force, the better—even though a young force is necessarily a relatively inexperienced one. But, then, the value of experience in a military context has always been difficult to gauge. For one thing, conventional military power is measured more in terms of quantity than of quality; the number of ground combat divisions has constituted a common yardstick of military power in the post–World War II period. As a result, the need to find the precise relationship between experience—as a measure of personnel quality—and military effectiveness has not been pressing. The advent of sophisticated work

3. U.S. Department of the Army, *Army Regulation 40-501*, Change 31, May 27, 1976, p. 9-3.

measurement methods based on industrial engineering and advanced statistical techniques has enabled the services to improve their estimates of quantitative personnel requirements, but determining the level of experience or skill that personnel should have continues to be based largely on judgment.

Thus it is not surprising that many military personnel policies pertaining to youth and vigor have apparently also been matters of judgment. According to one defense official: "The judgment that has been made in the Air Force is that we need a young vigorous force at the point of combat. . . . That is why we have opted for a system that does bring young, vigorous men into that position."[4] An Army spokesman extended the concept well beyond the direct labor of war: "War, in general, is a young man's game, whether you are leading a platoon, or whether you are running a medical unit, or whether you are running a depot in the overseas theater."[5]

Upward Mobility

Another factor that shapes the age composition of the military work force is the system of rank, a unique framework for personnel management that distinguishes the military establishment from all civilian organizations. Since rank indicates order of precedence, it holds a special importance for members of the armed forces. The perquisites and social status associated with higher military rank are well known; RHIP (rank has its privileges) has become almost cliché in the military community. For these reasons military personnel consider rank, and particularly the rate of advancement through the ranks, as the single most important measure of individual achievement. Manpower planners and policymakers accordingly place great emphasis on the promotion system. Indeed, the provision of reasonable and highly visible opportunity to advance through the ranks has come to be the centerpiece of the armed forces' personnel management systems.

To some extent the use of rank in the military could be compared with the use of civil service ratings in federal employment; both serve the pur-

4. Testimony of David P. Taylor, Assistant Secretary of the Air Force, in *Defense Officer Personnel Management Act,* Hearings before the Subcommittee on Manpower and Personnel of the Senate Committee on Armed Services, 94 Cong. 1 sess. (Government Printing Office, 1976), p. 122.

5. Testimony of Paul D. Phillips, Deputy Assistant Secretary of the Army for Manpower and Reserve Affairs, in ibid., p. 123.

pose of linking pay levels to job tasks. Similar arrangements, though less formal and only internally observed, are made by most large organizations, public or private. The principal difference, however, is that in the armed forces the ordering of skill levels is explicit rather than subsumed in job titles. Thus, for example, a person with the rank of master sergeant (pay grade E-8) could be employed as a supervisor in an aircraft maintenance unit or as a chef in a food service facility. And because the skill level would be considered equivalent in each case, the master sergeant would receive the same pay in either capacity for a given length of service in the force.

This arrangement is in part the legacy of an era during which the military was composed mainly of combat soldiers backed up by small numbers of support troops. Under these circumstances rank was based almost solely on seniority. At present the complex occupational structure of the armed services reinforces the need for a skill classification system applicable to personnel in all the major military occupational areas,[6] especially since military personnel are likely to engage in more than one occupation during their term of service. Rank, then, is probably intended to serve as an index of skill achievement independently of differences in occupational tasks. As such, this system is well in accordance with the long tradition of egalitarianism in the armed forces, since it guarantees equal rates of pay to personnel of the same rank, regardless of occupational specialty. Implicit is the assumption that all military tasks contribute equally to the attainment of force readiness.

Adherence to a system based on rank does not in itself necessarily contribute to the armed forces' very heavy dependence on young personnel, but in combination with the closed nature of the military system, predetermined promotion opportunities do strongly influence the average age of service personnel. In the private sector and to a somewhat lesser extent the federal civilian work force, employees move in and out of the organization at all skill levels and pay is vested in the job. Virtually all military people, however, enter at the bottom of the grade structure, are trained within the military, and progress through a sequence of career-broadening assignments and a hierarchy of skill levels, with their rank and pay following them.

An upward flow through the closed system at rates that the services consider necessary to maintain traditional pyramid-shaped organizational

---

6. The occupational structure of the armed forces is discussed in chapter 3.

structures has important implications for personnel turnover. It means that experienced people must continuously exit from the system to make room for those coming behind them; this in turn means that to maintain a constant strength a steady flow of new recruits must be fed into the system.

The net result has been a military establishment characterized by a large contingent of relatively inexperienced first-term personnel; only a small proportion of these serve beyond their initial tour. Once a person is in the career force, advancement through the ranks depends on personnel losses; many of these losses occur at 20 years of service, the point at which military retirement becomes vested. In fact, the military's early retirement provisions have been justified partly on the basis of the need to maintain a viable promotion system.

To illustrate, at the end of fiscal year 1977, 58.6 percent of the 1.8 million enlisted personnel in the armed forces had served four years or less. During the year about 407,500 personnel were lost to the rolls, with 78 percent of them departing either before or upon completion of their first enlistment period. To maintain authorized strengths, the services brought about 411,000 personnel into the enlisted ranks—a turnover rate of roughly 23 percent.[7]

Although by law the armed services may recruit volunteers up to 35 years of age, relatively few have been out of their teens. For example, during fiscal year 1977 approximately 70 percent of all volunteers were under 20 years of age, with the median at 18.9 years. This may be explained partly by the economics of the marketplace; the armed forces cannot bid for the services of skilled civilian technicians, since pay and promotion opportunities are tied to longevity in the service. But even under conscription, when older men could have been drafted, the armed forces considered young recruits more desirable, at least partly because of the problems perceived to be associated with age-authority inversions. Commenting on World War II experience, one research group concluded:

It is conducive to neither individual nor group morale to have an eighteen-year-old sergeant or a twenty-year-old lieutenant command a group composed of much older men. Effective group performance usually requires some limitation on the age range of its members and particularly in the age structure of superiors and subordinates.[8]

7. Based on unpublished data from the Office of the Assistant Secretary of Defense for Manpower, Reserve Affairs, and Logistics.

8. Eli Ginzberg and others, *The Lost Divisions,* The Ineffective Soldier: Lessons for Management and the Nation (Columbia University Press, 1959), p. 66.

Youth as "Free Goods"

The traditional preference of the military services for a youthful force became a legitimate need in the 1940s. After World War II the United States confronted the prospect of maintaining a large peacetime military establishment for the first time in its history. Coupled with an unprecedented requirement for postwar occupation forces, the perceived danger to U.S. security posed by the Communist Bloc and the preoccupation of the latter with massive ground formations established a pattern that had important consequences for the structure of U.S. military forces. To offset the threat without imposing a great and probably unpopular burden on the nation's economy, a large but relatively youthful force was institutionalized through conscription.

The military draft, which existed continuously between 1940 and 1973 except for a brief hiatus in the late 1940s, made the cost advantage of a young military force particularly striking. An almost endless reservoir of young draft-eligible males was available, and except for the relatively small and generally fixed costs of maintaining the selective service system, few expenses were involved in the procurement of manpower. Because conscription was justified mainly on the basis of patriotism and moral indebtedness to the nation, military pay was inordinately low, particularly in the lower grades. Thus young draftees were essentially viewed as free goods.

By creating a new and seemingly costless source of military manpower, the draft reinforced the belief that a younger force is a cheaper force.[9] It also made the costs of sustaining the career force more visible. First, older personnel command a level of compensation higher than that of their younger counterparts. Less obvious but just as real are the other financial costs exacted by older employees. For example, careerists are more likely to earn entitlement to retirement benefits and to have more dependents on the average than younger people, thus giving rise to higher

9. Critics of the conscription system have argued that the true economic cost imposed on the draftees is substantial and inequitably borne in the form of an implicit tax. The magnitude of the cost has been described as "the difference between the earnings the draftee or draft-motivated (reluctant) volunteer receives from the military (including income in kind) and the earnings that would just cause that individual to be willing to enter the military." See Larry A. Sjaastad and Ronald W. Hansen, "The Conscription Tax: An Empirical Analysis," *Studies Prepared for the President's Commission on an All-Volunteer Armed Force* (GPO, 1971), vol. 2, p. 4-1-2.

medical, housing, travel, and other dependent-related costs. Finally, and more significantly, additional monetary incentives are generally needed to sustain the career force through reenlistments.

While the draft neither eliminated nor directly met the quantitative needs of the services for careerists, it held the costs of sustaining the career force down; the annual steady flow of new recruits served to expand and continuously replenish the pool of potential reenlistees, thus containing the costs of reenlistment. It mattered little that a military force with a large concentration of young conscripts had a high rate of turnover. The cost of turnover is low when training is cheap. Coming out of World War II the military—particularly the ground forces—was geared for a replay of that conflict and continued to train recruits in accordance with its needs for relatively unskilled labor. Hence inexpensive training made high turnover attractive. Under these conditions a young force was viewed as a bargain.

Viability of the Reserve Forces

U.S. reserve forces have enjoyed the spin-off effects of the high turnover of personnel in the active forces. In addition to the direct recruitment of civilians, the reserve establishment has depended on an input of experienced personnel who leave the active forces. Upon entering the active forces recruits incur a six-year total service obligation; those who serve less than six years on active duty are required to serve the remaining time in a reserve unit in which they train periodically and are paid or as individuals who neither train nor get paid but are subject to call-up.[10]

As long as conscription was in effect the reserve components had no problems procuring manpower. They were not only being fed large numbers of experienced personnel leaving the active forces, but many civilians enlisted directly into the reserves to avoid the draft. In fact, since active duty obligations were of short duration (many for just two years), a large proportion of those leaving active duty had a relatively long reserve obligation.

The end of the draft in 1973 had a profound effect on reserve recruitment. Organized units, especially those in the Army reserve components, have had difficulty in meeting their authorized strength levels. This has been partly due to increases in the average length of the initial term of

10. The Armed Forces Reserve Act of 1952 provides a complex patchwork of active and reserve options for fulfilling the six-year obligation.

active service, with corresponding decreases in the average length of time spent fulfilling a reserve obligation.[11] This shrinkage has prompted some to recommend shorter active duty enlistment periods so as to increase turnover, thereby expanding the pool of potential reservists. Others have called for a return to conscription or for the institution of some form of national service.

The Military and Society

Social arguments have also been made in support of the large personnel turnover that characterizes a youthful military force. A large steady flow of people into the military, most of whom serve for only one term, has been considered a means to guard against the development of a separate military ethos. In this respect citizen soldiers are viewed as an important link between the military and society. Some scholars who stress the necessity of a broad ideological balance conclude that "the military should treat high rates of turnover *after one complete tour of duty* as a sign of organizational success rather than failure."[12]

The benefits of large turnover have also been gauged in terms of the contribution to society of the military's role as a training institution. Operating the nation's largest single vocational training program, each year the armed forces offer an opportunity to acquire skills and knowledge that will not only enable thousands of people to carry out their military duties but in many instances will also prepare them for more productive careers in the civilian sector. Often these opportunities for job training and educational assistance are not available elsewhere, particularly to disadvantaged youth.

Over the years countless high school dropouts have entered the military, earned diplomas, learned marketable skills, and returned to civilian life as more productive members of society. Some observers stress the importance of the military's role in this process and urge continuation of that role.

Public responsibilities and concern for the individuals involved dictate that the military act as a human resource development agency providing training

11. Also influencing the decline has been the large increase in the proportion of personnel who, for administrative reasons, do not complete their first term of enlistment and who are also released from their reserve obligation.

12. Jerald G. Bachman, John D. Blair, and David R. Segal, *The All-Volunteer Force: A Study of Ideology in the Military* (University of Michigan Press, 1977), p. 147. Emphasis in the original.

for high turnover workers not only to make them productive during their service tenure but also to ease their transition to civilian life with a minimum of social friction and personal loss.[13]

THE MILITARY'S involvement with the nation's youth is largely the result of the factors discussed above. All in all the practice has served the nation well and, given the conditions under which the system evolved, would continue to serve U.S. national security purposes. In recent years, however, fundamental changes in American society in general and in the military establishment in particular have cast doubt on the expediency of prevailing military manpower utilization policies, some of which are anchored in long tradition. One of these is the accent on youth.

13. Sar A. Levitan and Karen Cleary Alderman, *Warriors at Work: The Volunteer Armed Force,* Sage Library of Social Research, 58 (Sage Publications, 1977), p. 199.

CHAPTER THREE

YOUTH, EXPERIENCE,
AND EFFECTIVENESS

ADVANCES IN TECHNOLOGY over the past quarter of a century have had a dramatic influence on the U.S. defense establishment. Unlike the armed forces of earlier eras that were dominated by combat operatives— infantrymen, tank crews, artillerymen, aircrewmen, and fighting ships' companies—the vast majority of military personnel today are involved in supporting the combat mission.

The ascendancy of technicians and specialists over warriors that has been the result of technological substitution has yielded a more industrialized military institution, a large segment of which closely resembles civilian organizations. Among the many questions brought to the fore by this transformation is the relevance of military manpower policies and practices that emphasize youthfulness at the expense of experience. This chapter examines the nature of today's military jobs and assesses the relative importance of youth and experience to the performance of those jobs.

Technological and Organizational Change

In many ways research and development for military purposes have been forerunners of commercial and industrial applications, at times serving to accelerate the overall pace of technological substitution. And as the weapons of war have become more sophisticated, so too have the skills necessary to operate and maintain them.

Major Trends

A century ago U.S. military forces consisted mainly of Army and Marine Corps infantrymen and Navy "ablebodied" seamen.[1] During the

1. The first five paragraphs of this section draw heavily on Harold Wool, *The Military Specialist: Skilled Manpower for the Armed Forces* (Johns Hopkins Press,

Civil War, for example, the vast majority (95 percent) of Union soldiers were basic riflemen or were in associated combat units; only a few were engaged in support activities such as repairing guns, wagons, and saddles. The Navy of that era, consisting mainly of wooden sailing ships and some crude ironclads, also had limited demands for skilled specialists. By and large the principal duties involved manning sails, handling ropes, and standing watch; by one estimate the deck force of a typical sailing frigate comprised close to 90 percent of the entire enlisted crew. The few specialists that were required possessed such skills as sailmaker, carpenter, cooper, and armorer.

Mechanization in the military followed the advent of the industrial revolution and was slow in developing. It was first manifested in the Navy, which began to depend on steam as early as 1815, but modern steam-powered, steel-plated ships were not introduced until the 1880s. These new warships equipped with a variety of mechanical and electrical systems created new demands for specialists. The percentage of the ships' companies detailed to general deck work declined to about 55 percent, and the remainder were assigned to engineer or craftsmen duties. The Army was slower to adapt to technological advances. As late as the Spanish-American War, about nine of every ten Army enlisted men were in combat units.

More dramatic transformations in weapon systems occurred during World War I and had the most pronounced impact on the Army. The combined effects of the introduction of motorized transport, military aircraft, and armored fighting vehicles, on the one hand, and the logistics demands imposed by a "foreign" war, on the other, were striking. By the end of the war the traditional doughboy was in a numerical minority. Almost 60 percent of all enlisted men were in noncombat jobs; about half of these were employed as craftsmen, mechanics and repairmen, administrative and clerical personnel, and technicians. As Harold Wool, a former defense official, has described the situation: "Behind the 'man with the gun' was a complex array of support units of all types . . . manned by personnel who, though in uniform, performed duties generally paralleling in occupational context those performed by workers in the civilian economy."[2]

1968), chaps. 2 and 3. Wool's book, based on first-hand experience as a manpower official in the Pentagon, is one of the seminal works in the field of military manpower utilization.

   2. Ibid., p. 15.

The pace of technological development in the military slowed between the wars, but major advances occurred in aviation, ground vehicles, communications, and other support activities. And by the end of World War II, Wool observed, the military specialist had come of age. About 75 percent of military enlisted personnel were in occupations *not* involving ground combat operations. Only 39 percent of Army and 34 percent of Marine Corps enlisted jobs were classified as "ground combat"; moreover, fewer than half of these were infantry billets. And as marked as the technological changes between the Civil War and World War II had been, they have been dwarfed by subsequent innovations. The spectacular evolution of thermonuclear weapons; the dramatic developments in aircraft systems; the unprecedented advances in computer-based command, control, and communications; and finally, the introduction of space technology have imposed even greater requirements on the armed forces for skilled manpower.

Although the military's rolls had included skilled technicians before the 1940s, Wool noted that "the outbreak of World War II found the personnel systems of the Military Services poorly prepared to cope with the vast needs for specialized manpower generated by World War II."[3] As the war wore on, the armed forces began to develop procedures for identifying military personnel by function and by occupational specialty; by mid-1944, for example, the Army occupational classification system identified 873 different military occupational specialties and 487 civilian-type specialties. By 1947 the following broad military occupational areas had been established by the Department of Defense for cross-reference and personnel classification purposes:

> Ground combat
> Electronics
> Other technical
> Administrative and clerical
> Mechanics and repairmen
> Craftsmen
> Services

As the range of military specialties widened, the number of major occupational areas increased and job titles were revised to reflect the ever-increasing complexity of military jobs. Mainly as a result of the growing number of technical military specialties, the category of jobs previously called "other technical" was divided into three separate categories: com-

3. Ibid., p. 19.

munications and intelligence; medical and dental; and other technical. The following categories are currently in use:[4]

> Infantry, gun crews, and seamanship specialists
>
> Electronic equipment repairmen
>
> Communications and intelligence specialists
>
> Medical and dental specialists
>
> Other technical and allied specialists
>
> Functional support and administration
>
> Electrical/mechanical equipment repairmen
>
> Craftsmen
>
> Service and supply handlers

The evolution in the mix of jobs in the armed forces can be traced with the aid of table 3-1, which presents the distribution of trained enlisted personnel by major occupational category in 1945, 1957, and 1977. In this table military occupational areas are classified so as to correspond roughly to civilian occupational categories.[5] The overall growth in the proportion of personnel trained in white-collar occupations is particularly evident, reflecting the shift away from work requiring general skills toward that requiring special skills. White-collar workers in the military

4. Each major occupational area contains more detailed occupational groups and sub-groups. The Department of Defense establishes the major occupational areas and each service develops its own individual job titles within these areas. Conversion tables are used to tie each job in one service to a similar or related job, if one exists, in each of the other services. This cross-classification of jobs serves as an "occupational coding structure," as "a guide to the Office of the Secretary of Defense in manpower management and policy planning, to the Military Departments for various personnel administration functions, and as a basis for statistical reports." (U.S. Department of Defense, Office of the Assistant Secretary of Defense for Manpower, Reserve Affairs, and Logistics, *Occupational Conversion Manual: Enlisted Officer/Civilian,* December 1977 [DOD, Defense Manpower Data Center, 1977], p. I. At the enlisted level, about 2,000 military and 275 civilian occupations are now classified in the manual.)

5. The occupational classification system developed by the Bureau of the Census has 12 major occupational categories; these are broken down further into over 400 occupations (see U.S. Bureau of the Census, *Census of Population, 1970,* Subject Reports: *Occupational Characteristics,* Final Report PC(2)-7A [Government Printing Office, 1973], p. IX.). Although the civilian and military classifications differ in some respects, for many purposes—and those of this study in particular—the two systems yield valuable comparative information. The establishment of comparability between the major civilian and military occupations has been attempted elsewhere at different levels of aggregation (see *Studies Prepared for the President's Commission on an All-Volunteer Armed Force,* November 1970 [GPO, 1971], especially vol. 1, pts. 1 and 2). Building on this approach, the present study focuses on broadly comparable military and civilian major occupational categories.

Table 3-1. Distribution of Trained Military Enlisted Personnel by Major Occupational Category, Selected Years

Major occupational category[a]	Percent of trained enlisted personnel		
	1945	1957	1977
White-collar	**28**	**40**	**46**
Technical workers[b]	13	21	28
Clerical workers[c]	15	19	18
Blue-collar	**72[d]**	**60**	**55**
Craftsmen[e]	29	32	27
Service and supply workers	17	13	12
Infantry, gun crews, and seamanship specialists	24	15	16

Sources: Data for 1945 and 1957 from Harold Wool, *The Military Specialist: Skilled Manpower for the Armed Forces* (Johns Hopkins Press, 1968), table III-3, p. 42. Data for 1977 provided by Office of the Assistant Secretary of Defense for Manpower, Reserve Affairs, and Logistics. Percentages are rounded.

a. Categories are based on the Department of Defense occupational classification system explained in the text.

b. Percentages for 1945 and 1957 include "electronics" and "other technical" categories. Percentage for 1977 includes "electronic equipment repairmen," "communications and intelligence specialists," "medical and dental specialists," and "other technical and allied specialists" categories.

c. Percentages for 1945 and 1957 include administrative and clerical personnel. Percentage for 1977 is for the "functional support and administration" category.

d. Includes 2 percent classified as miscellaneous.

e. Percentages for 1945 and 1957 include "mechanics and repairmen" and "craftsmen" categories. Percentage for 1977 includes "electrical/mechanical equipment repairmen" and "craftsmen" categories.

now make up 46 percent of the total versus 28 percent in 1945, well in line with the growth of white-collar employment in the economy as a whole. The data show that in the military the change has occurred mainly in the technical fields, which now require computer specialists; teletype and electronic instrument technicians; radio systems operators; translators and interpreters; medical technologists, health technicians, and dental specialists; photographers; draftsmen; meteorologists; and a variety of other analysts and laboratory technicians.[6] And even though the percentage of clerical personnel has remained relatively stable over the years, it could be argued that special-skills requirements are now probably imposed even on these workers, many of whom must be familiar with the use and operation of data processing systems.

Among blue-collar enlisted workers, who now constitute 55 percent of the military labor force, compared with 72 percent in 1945, similar shifts have occurred, mainly owing to the sharp decrease in the percentage of ground combat soldiers during the decade following World War II. At present craftsmen account for 27 percent of all enlisted workers and about half of all blue-collar military personnel. By contrast, only 40 per-

6. Department of Defense, *Occupational Conversion Manual*, pp. 15–48.

Table 3-2. Distribution of Trained Enlisted Personnel by Major Occupational Category and Service, Selected Years

Percent

Major occupational category[a]	Army 1945	Army 1957	Army 1977	Navy 1945	Navy 1957	Navy 1977	Marine Corps 1945	Marine Corps 1957	Marine Corps 1977	Air Force 1945	Air Force 1957	Air Force 1977
White-collar	**25**	**34**	**41**	**30**	**36**	**48**	**27**	**31**	**34**	**36**	**51**	**55**
Technical workers	10	18	24	19	26	36	12	10	17	16	23	32
Clerical workers	15	16	17	11	10	12	15	21	17	20	28	23
Blue-collar	**74**	**66**	**59**	**71**	**64**	**52**	**73**	**69**	**66**	**65**	**49**	**46**
Craftsmen	16	19	18	60	56	40	24	19	21	41	37	30
Service and supply workers	19	16	12	11	8	7	15	11	15	14	12	14
Infantry, gun crews, and seamanship specialists[b]	39	31	29	...	...	5	34	39	30	10	...	2

Sources: Data for 1945 and 1957 are from Harold Wool, *The Military Specialist: Skilled Manpower for the Armed Forces* (Johns Hopkins Press, 1968), table III-4, p. 43. Data for 1977 were provided by the Office of the Assistant Secretary of Defense for Manpower, Reserve Affairs, and Logistics. Percentages are rounded.

a. Defined in notes in table 3-1.

b. The roster of specialties included in this category has changed over the years. For example, boatswains' mates are now considered to be seamanship specialists; in earlier years they were not included in any category of occupations requiring training.

cent of blue-collar workers were craftsmen in 1945. Currently, the duties of enlisted craftsmen involve "the maintenance and repair of electrical, mechanical, hydraulic and pneumatic equipment," and "the formulation, fabrication, and installation of structures and components, the installation and maintenance of utilities, and related trades and crafts."[7] Military personnel working in these jobs perform tasks similar to those of mechanics and repairmen, boilermakers, construction craftsmen, blacksmiths, plumbers and pipefitters, shipfitters, electricians, printing craftsmen, machinists, and even those of bakers and tailors in the civilian sector.

The armed services have always differed significantly in their occupational structures, and despite technological advancement interservice differences are still apparent. Unlike the Navy and the Air Force, the Army and the Marine Corps have always "specialized" in combat-related operations. In the former two the nature of the major capital inputs—ships and aircraft—has created different manpower requirements. Ships must be largely self-sufficient and self-contained units over long periods of time and thus require a high proportion of craftsmen and technicians for maintenance and repair, and aircraft are almost wholly dependent on ground support facilities.

Even so, the impact of technological change is evident in all the services. Table 3-2 shows the distribution of trained enlisted personnel by major occupational area and by service in 1945, 1957, and 1977. Note the substantial growth in the number of white-collar workers over the past 32 years in the Navy and the Air Force in particular; the proportion of trained technicians has almost doubled from 19 to 36 percent, and from 16 to 32 percent, respectively. Significantly, the Army in relative terms has experienced an even greater increase in the percentage of technical specialists, which now account for almost a quarter of all enlisted soldiers. In the Marine Corps the change has been less pronounced but, still, the proportion of leathernecks trained for combat-related jobs declined by nearly 10 percentage points to 30 percent of the total between 1957 and 1977.

Current Occupational Mix

To accomplish their mission, the armed forces are now relying on a diversified labor force, which as table 3-3 shows, performs many of the

7. Ibid., pp. 3–4.

Table 3-3. Distribution of Civilian Sector Workers and Military Enlisted Personnel by Occupational Category, 1977
Percent

Occupational category	Civilian sector workers		Military personnel	
	Total	Male	Total[a]	Enlisted
Common to both sectors				
Technical	15[b]	15[b]	30[b]	28[e]
Managers and administrators	10	14	3	[d]
Clerical workers	18	6	15	18[e]
Craftsmen	13	21	23	27[f]
Service workers	14	9	10	12[g]
Mainly confined to one sector				
Tactical operations officers and infantry, gun crews, and seamanship specialists	...	...	19	16
Farm workers	3	4	...	...
Sales workers	6	6	...	...
Other (operatives and nonfarm workers)	20	25	...	...

Sources: Unpublished data provided by the Office of the Assistant Secretary of Defense for Manpower, Reserve Affairs, and Logistics; and U.S. Department of Labor, Bureau of Labor Statistics, *Employment and Earnings*, vol. 25 (May 1978), table A-22, p. 35. Percentages are rounded.

a. Includes officers. General officers and executives; administrators; and supply, procurement, and allied officers are classified as managers and administrators. Intelligence; engineering and maintenance; and scientific, professional, and medical officers are classified as professional workers. The classification of the enlisted personnel is explained in the notes below.

b. Includes professional workers.

c. Includes electronic equipment repairmen, communications and intelligence specialists, medical and dental specialists, and other technical and allied specialists.

d. To some extent a few enlisted positions may involve administrative duties, apart from the supervisory responsibilities of staff at the E-8 and E-9 grade levels. However, because it is difficult to distinguish between supervisors and administrators among enlisted personnel, and because officers include a relatively well-defined class of managers and administrators in the military, it is assumed here—perhaps at the risk of oversimplification—that managerial positions are normally filled by officers.

e. The "functional support and administration" category.

f. Includes "electrical/mechanical equipment repairmen" and "craftsmen" categories.

g. The "service and supply handlers" category.

tasks usually associated with civilian employment. It is interesting to note that despite the absence of sales, managerial, and some blue-collar (noncraftsmen) personnel from the enlisted force, the military depends more heavily on technicians and craftsmen than does the civilian sector—that is, on personnel trained in a wide variety of modern specialties hardly fitting old stereotypes.[8]

8. While the data in table 3-3 allow for meaningful comparison of the occupational structures in the military and civilian sectors at a high level of aggregation, they are not without limitations. The Census Bureau's criteria for grouping occupations together sometimes differ from the criteria used by the Defense Department. For example, clerical occupations in the military include computer programmers and some analysts who would normally be classified as technical in the Census Bureau's system. Since these specialists account for only a small proportion of clerical personnel, no attempt has been made to regroup the data.

The changes in the military occupational structure and in the skill composition of defense manpower resemble the occupational shifts that have occurred in the civilian sector, where technological advancement has similarly been manifested in the growing proportion of the labor force concentrated in the technical and craftsmen occupations. As a result of mechanization and automation, employment in two labor-intensive occupations, each unique to its sector, declined: the armed forces have come to rely less and less on infantry, and the civilian economy witnessed a dramatic fall in the proportion of the labor force engaged in agriculture —from 13 percent in 1947 to only 3 percent in 1976.[9]

The data in table 3-3 indicate that contrary to perceived stereotypes, not only do the defense and civilian sectors have a significant number of occupations in common, but the proportion of technical and craft workers is greater in the military. In particular, the percentage of technical enlisted jobs is almost twice as large in the armed forces as in the rest of the economy. Over a quarter of all enlisted positions fall in the category of crafts, while only 13 percent of civilian workers are craftsmen; and even when only the male civilian work force is considered, still only about a fifth of its members are employed as craftsmen.

These figures are instructive inasmuch as they reveal a considerable occupational overlap between the military and the civilian sectors. As real and inevitable as this overlap may appear, it troubles some observers who believe that it also signifies the erosion of the institutional format of the armed forces—an erosion that may be socially undesirable. Charles C. Moskos, Jr., has observed that

. . . the ascendant occupational model in the armed forces alerts one to, and makes sense out of, current organizational trends in the social structure of the military. If there is concern with current developments—the possibility of trade unionism, excessive reliance on contract civilians, service morale, and the like—then attention ought to be focused on the root cause and not just on the overt symptoms.[10]

And Moskos fears that these trends "can lead to complete occupationalism, with a resultant confusion of the military role, internally and externally."[11]

9. *Employment and Training Report of the President, 1977* (GPO, 1977), table A-1, p. 135.
10. Charles C. Moskos, Jr., "From Institution to Occupation: Trends in Military Organization," *Armed Forces and Society,* vol. 4 (Fall 1977), p. 48.
11. Charles C. Moskos, Jr., "Compensation and the Military Institution," *Air Force Magazine,* vol. 61 (April 1978), p. 35.

Others, however, would interpret these trends merely as evidence of an institution in transition. According to Morris Janowitz:

The military profession is undergoing long-term transformation which involves increased penetration by other professions and institutions. . . .

The formulation of the shift from institution to occupation sounds to me to have overtones of an ideological appeal to return to the "good old days." But there is no return, although there is much to be learned about the transmission of the viable aspects of tradition and the record of adaptation.[12]

Current Occupational Requirements

Military manpower policies have been based on the claim that "youth and vigor" are by far the most important qualificat'ons for military service. But how valid is this claim? The military has opted for a youthful force, judging it better able to endure the hardships of military duty and hence more effective in maintaining defense readiness. However, although the proportion of physically arduous military jobs, notably the combat-related positions, has been declining, in relative terms the contingent of military personnel under the age of 24 is about as large today as in 1950 (table 2-2). This seeming inconsistency calls for a reexamination of the more fundamental issue of the relationship between youthfulness, job performance, and military effectiveness. This relationship in which age is a proxy for physical fitness is neither as clear nor as simple as that implied by past and current military manpower policies.

The Physical Factor

Effective performance in some military jobs obviously demands physical strength and endurance; yet these jobs account for a small proportion of the total, and physical standards have been neither well defined nor rigorously applied.[13] The prevailing doctrine, based on several decades of experience, assumes that persons capable of meeting minimum medical standards will also be able to acquire a level of physical fitness during basic military training that will qualify them for any job specialty. While physical fitness is not precisely defined, it is usually considered to encom-

12. Morris Janowitz, "From Institutional to Occupational: The Need for Conceptual Continuity," *Armed Forces and Society,* vol. 4 (Fall 1977), pp. 53–54.

13. This section is from Martin Binkin and Shirley J. Bach, *Women and the Military* (Brookings Institution, 1977), pp. 78–80, 82.

pass some combination of strength, endurance, flexibility, balance, speed, agility, and power.

MEDICAL ENTRANCE EXAMS. The examination process to ascertain whether enlistees meet prescribed medical standards includes the usual clinical examination of the body, laboratory tests, and physical measurements (for example, height, weight, and blood pressure). On the basis of this examination the physician identifies any disqualifying defects, and evaluates the examinee's functional capacity. The evaluation—a physician's subjective assessment of an individual's ability to perform military duties—is quantified in a "physical profile," a device once used by all the services but now by only the Army and the Air Force to communicate an examinee's general physical condition to nonmedical personnel. The profile is intended to serve as an index of overall functional capacity; therefore, the functional capacity of a particular organ or system of the body, rather than any defect per se, is evaluated. The examining physician assigns a grade on a numerical scale from 1 to 4 to six factors representing the major human functions. The factors now used by the Army are (1) physical capacity or stamina, (2) upper extremities, (3) lower extremities, (4) hearing and ear defects, (5) eyes, and (6) psychiatric. Together these factors provide what is commonly called the PULHES profile. (The Air Force, as explained below, has added another factor.)

Grade 1 signifies a high level of medical fitness; for example, assigned to the "physical capacity" factor, it indicates good muscular development and an ability to perform maximum effort for indefinite periods. Grade 2 indicates that a medical condition or physical defect may impose certain job limitations and is assigned to those who are able to perform maximum effort over long periods. Grade 3 signals a moderate defect and is given to a person who is unable to perform maximum effort except for brief or moderate periods. Finally, Grade 4 indicates that a person is below minimum standards for enlistment. Until recently examinees have not been required to demonstrate measurable physical strength and endurance.

Scores assigned to each factor are combined to form a profile serial number. Under current Army personnel procurement standards two categories of enlistees are acceptable for peacetime duty. First, those with a PULHES profile serial "111111," signifying no demonstrable anatomical or physiological impairment within established standards, are considered medically fit and can generally be assigned without limitations. The other acceptable group includes those whose profile serial contains a Grade 2 as the lowest designator. For example, slightly limited mobility of joints or muscular weakness are acceptable, and the enlistee is rendered combat fit, with no significant assignment limitations. In general, grades 3 and 4 assigned to any factor are disqualifying for initial entrance but are acceptable for someone already in the service.[14]

MEDICAL FINDINGS AND JOB REQUIREMENTS. The relationship between medical examination results and the physical requirements associated with specific jobs has varied by service. The Navy and the Marine Corps do not use the PULHES profile for classification purposes, and neither service has established physical standards for specific jobs. The Army, on the other hand, associates a profile serial with each specialty. For example, entrance into the infantry career field requires a perfect profile—"111111" (or "picket fence" in military jargon)—but a "222221" profile is acceptable for, say, a missile electronics repairman, who must attain the highest score only in the psychiatric factor. Finally, the Air Force has taken the lead in experimenting with better measures of physical strength and began to establish more specific standards as early as 1973. Each specialty was classified according to the type of work involved, ranging from "sedentary work" (lifting 10 pounds maximum) to "very heavy" ("lifting objects in excess of 100 pounds with frequent lifting or carrying of objects weighing up to 50 pounds").[15] These specifications, however, served merely as a guide for assigning personnel; assignment was not determined by a test of lifting ability alone but continued to be based on the physician's judgment.

MEASUREMENT OF PHYSICAL CAPACITY. In recent years pressures imposed by the expanded role of women have prompted the Pentagon to seriously consider establishing more exact physical standards and developing techniques for measuring a person's ability to meet such standards. The Air Force, playing a pioneer role, added a seventh item—the "X" factor—to the PULHES profile in 1976.[16] The grade assigned to this factor is based on a demonstrated ability to lift a certain weight to a certain height. For example, according to the Air Force, lifting 70 pounds to a height of six feet (Grade 1) indicates an ability to perform "maximum heavy duty over prolonged periods." Lifting 40 pounds to elbow

14. U.S. Department of the Army, *Army Regulation 40-501,* Change 31, May 27, 1976, pp. 9-3–9-5.

15. U.S. Department of the Air Force, *Air Force Manual 39-1,* vol. 1, Change 14, Attachment 57, September 5, 1973, p. A57-1.

16. The change was instituted by the Air Force in *Air Force Regulation 160-43,* Attachment 2, June 21, 1976.

height (Grade 2) means that an enlistee can perform "sustained moderate duty over prolonged periods." Finally, those able to lift only 20 pounds to elbow height (Grade 3) are considered to be capable of performing "standard light duty over normal work periods."[17]

The Air Force has also identified the minimum grade required for each occupation. Of 330 enlisted career fields, 24 require Grade 1; 197, Grade 2; and 109, Grade 3. Almost half of the 400,000 enlisted jobs are in the moderate duty category, while only about 63,000, or 16 percent of the total, require heavy physical activity; the remaining 140,000, or 35 percent, are in the light physical duty category.[18]

The Air Force program is an experiment. Whether this single-dimensional, relatively simple measurement is a valid common denominator for predicting physical fitness is still under review. While continuing to observe the results of the Air Force program, the other services apparently have undertaken independent research to relate the physical capacities of men and women to classes of jobs.[19]

Until that research is completed, the precise total number of jobs that might require extraordinary physical prowess cannot be measured. A rough estimate is provided within the occupational classification system, however. One major occupational area, "infantry, gun crews, and seamanship specialists," includes a rather heterogeneous grouping of jobs that appear to have only two things in common. First, at least as far as the Army and the Marine Corps are concerned, they involve tasks that are generally thought of as combat related, and second, they can generally be performed by those who, although not highly skilled, are physically fit. Thus some 250,000 jobs included in this category can be considered an upper bound on the number of jobs for which physical fitness can undeniably be imposed as a job requirement.[20]

17. Department of the Air Force, *Air Force Regulation 160-43*, Attachment 2.

18. U.S. Department of the Air Force, *Air Force Manual 39-1*, vol. 2, Change 23, Attachment 57, April 26, 1976, and data provided by the Department of the Air Force.

19. It is worth noting that problems in defining physical requirements and devising valid predictive measures of physical performance are not confined to the armed forces. Wide variations can be observed in the physical agility tests being used by the nation's police departments, ranging from emphasis on brute strength to emphasis on staying power. See Catherine Higgs Milton and others, *Women in Policing: A Manual* (Police Foundation, 1974), p. 13.

20. Admittedly this categorization is an attempt to simplify complex and poorly defined relationships, and it has inherent limitations. Obviously some jobs in this category—field artillery fire control specialists, for example—demand at least as much brain as brawn. The basic mental qualifications specified for these jobs by the

Age and Physical Capacity

Even in those cases where the need for peak physical conditioning is obvious, a further question can be posed. Are young people better able than their older counterparts to fulfill those requirements? The answer is far from clear. There is no single index to describe the aging process; although by most measures physical capacity appears to decay with age, the rates of decline indicated by the different measures vary widely.

For example, cardiac output and respiratory performance usually decline with age at a much greater rate than do neural activity and metabolic function. Even in these cases, however, the average forty-year-old possesses over 95 percent of the cardiac output and about 90 percent of the respiratory capacity of the average thirty-year-old.[21] In terms of performance in three classes of "speeded activities," research results indicate that the steepest loss as a function of age occurs in running events, which require 35 to 40 percent more time at age 60 than at age 20. The least loss due to age was evidenced in simple reaction time tasks, which were performed only 5 percent slower at age 60 than at age 20. The loss in both between the ages of 20 and 30 was negligible. Research results also suggest that maximal muscle strength is achieved between the ages of 25 and 30, gradually diminishing until age 50, after which a sharper decline occurs.[22]

This evidence led one research group to conclude:

Age undeniably has some effect on most, if not all, human capacities. In most instances, however, severe age-deficits are not found until the sixth, seventh, and eighth decades. In studies done on work performance through the usual work lifetime (age 20 to age 60), there is little if any evidence that older workers are not capable of performing equally well in most job situations. Exceptions would be those occupations, and they do exist within the military, which require superior visual acuity, strength, or reaction time.[23]

Army generally include "adaptability, decisiveness, emotional stability, attentiveness, reasoning ability, and a high degree of mechanical aptitude." (U.S. Department of the Army, *Army Regulation 611-201*, Change 2, July 1, 1974, p. 3-12-3.) On the other hand, jobs in other categories—construction, for example—would be at least as physically demanding as some in the so-called combat category.

21. James F. Parker, Jr., Diane G. Christensen, and Martin G. Every, *A Review of the "Youth and Vigor" Concept and Its Importance in Military Occupations*, Final Report submitted to the President's Commission on Military Compensation (Falls Church, Va.: BioTechnology, Inc., 1978), fig. 3, p. 10.

22. Ibid., pp. 5–10.

23. Ibid., p. 30.

How exceptional these occupations are, considering age-vigor requirements, is difficult to say with any degree of precision. Just how youthful should personnel manning these physically demanding jobs be? To the extent that a parallel involving age-vigor requirements (though certainly not overall purpose) can be drawn, it is useful to examine the utilization of manpower in the civilian sector. This does not imply that the military as an employer is faced with production goals similar to those of civilian employers; in fact, it is because these goals differ that the occupational structure of the military differs from that of the civilian sector. Nonetheless, similar worker skills are required for particular jobs regardless of the sector of employment. Moreover, since producing units in the civilian sector, unlike those in the defense establishment, are normally subject to market-imposed penalties (loss of sales and hence profits should they operate inefficiently), they are more likely to arrive at cost-effective decisions in hiring workers. Thus insight into civilian sector job-staffing practices is very useful.

In civilian jobs that have no direct counterparts in the military but may nevertheless involve considerable physical labor, age does not appear to be an obstacle to employment; for example, the median age for teamsters is 38.4 years, while for longshoremen and stevedores it is 44.3 years. And even civilian firemen and policemen (professions requiring physical characteristics not unlike those required of military personnel in the combat arms) are considerably older on the average than their counterparts in the defense area; the median age is about 36 years for policemen and 38 years for firemen.[24]

Important as it may be, then, the requirement for youthfulness and vigor is neither overwhelming nor applicable to all of the jobs in the military services.

The Experience Factor

The armed forces, however, do appear to have pressing needs in those occupational areas where expertise, rather than physical vigor and stamina, is critical for effective job performance. In general, experienced workers—naturally, older ones—are more productive workers and hence can perform better in their jobs. Experience acquired during the informal education process that almost every job involves is cumulative; on-the-

24. Data in this paragraph are from Bureau of the Census, *Census of Population, 1970: Occupational Characteristics,* table 1, pp. 9, 11.

job training, learning by trial and error, and repetition of tasks enable workers to improve their performance as they gain in know-how. For these reasons pay and promotions are generally linked to job tenure, and in most occupations older employees as a rule receive higher salaries than do their younger coworkers. The assumption that experience and productivity are positively related has long been implicit in most civilian pay systems and especially where remuneration arrangements are formalized, notably in the government.

In recent years the relationship among age, experience, productivity, and earnings of civilian workers has been systematically subjected to and substantially validated by numerous empirical tests.[25] Lacking a similarly comprehensive analysis in the defense area—where output and hence productivity are not readily quantifiable, much less measurable—is it fair to assume that experienced workers are equally important in a military setting? The answer to this question would depend on what tasks are actually involved in the military setting. To the extent that many of these tasks are not unique to the military and must be completed no less successfully than in a civilian setting, the expertise of older workers would seem to be at least equally valuable as a resource to the armed forces. Several prominent members of the defense establishment subscribe to this view. For example, the Military Compensation Policy Board drew the following parallel in 1967:

Those serving in higher work levels are generally older than those serving in lower work levels. . . . There is universal agreement that work level (military pay grade) is one proper basis for salary discrimination. Plant managers earn more than foremen because their work is expected to contribute more to attainment of the company's objectives than is the work of the foremen. Generals get paid more than second lieutenants because generals are expected to contribute more to accomplishment of the military's mission than are second lieutenants.[26]

25. See, for example, H. S. Houthakker, "Education and Income," *Review of Economics and Statistics,* vol. 41 (February 1959), pp. 24–28; and Giora Hanoch, "An Economic Analysis of Earnings and Schooling," *Journal of Human Resources,* vol. 2 (Summer 1967), pp. 310–29. In these and other studies the age-wage relationship is examined and wage profiles that show the rate of increase in earnings with age within various schooling groups are estimated. When age and experience are statistically separable, the positive effect of experience on earnings is more clearly isolated; this relationship is reported in Jacob Mincer, *Schooling, Experience and Earnings* (Distributed by Columbia University Press for National Bureau of Economic Research, 1974), especially chap. 4.

26. U.S. Department of Defense, *Modernizing Military Pay,* vol. 1: *Active Duty Compensation,* Report of the First Quadrennial Review of Military Compensation (DOD, 1967), pp. 100–101.

In 1976 the Defense Manpower Commission reported to the President and Congress:

In noncombat jobs, the maturity, experience, and judgement gained through longer service are more valuable than physical stamina and agility. . . . A longer maximum career is feasible for Service members in noncombat jobs, particularly for those in technical and professional jobs. A person in these jobs could normally serve effectively until age 60.[27]

And more recently Assistant Secretary of Defense John P. White said in testimony before a congressional committee: "Experienced people are more productive and are critical to the proper operation and maintenance of an increasingly complex military force."[28]

More and more, military managers are becoming aware of the need to enrich the experience mix of the enlisted force in order to improve its effectiveness. This concern is reflected in statements that acknowledge retention imbalances, even though they rarely refer to imbalances in the experience mix explicitly. The connection is clear in the following statement by Vice Admiral James D. Watkins:

Our most critical retention problems and shortfalls are [among] those personnel with generally seven to twelve years of service. . . . This shortfall, coupled with our existing experienced personnel shortages of about 16,000 in the 8–17th year of service at the end of FY 1977, significantly impact on fleet readiness.[29]

The extent of the impact was observed by Senator John Culver on a field inspection trip in 1976. Among his findings: (1) a major problem aboard the aircraft carrier *Constellation* was "the lack of adequate numbers of enlisted personnel for supervisory and training positions (E-4 and E-5 levels) which are necessary to reach a readiness proficiency"; (2) "shortages of key supervisory (E-5 to E-9) enlisted personnel in the machinist mate, boiler technician, and boatswain mate skills [were] a serious concern on the aircraft carriers in the Pacific Fleet"; and (3) for the Pacific Surface Fleet, "the major problem [appeared] to be from shortages in the

27. Defense Manpower Commission, *Defense Manpower: The Keystone of National Security,* Report to the President and the Congress, April 1976 (GPO, 1976), pp. 258–59.

28. Statement of John P. White, Assistant Secretary of Defense for Manpower, Reserve Affairs, and Logistics, in *Department of Defense Appropriations for 1979,* Hearings before a Subcommittee of the House Committee on Appropriations, 95 Cong. 2 sess. (GPO, 1978), p. 12.

29. Statement of Vice Admiral James D. Watkins, Chief of Naval Personnel and Deputy Chief of Naval Operations for Manpower, *Department of Defense Authorization for Appropriations for Fiscal Year 1979,* Hearings before the Senate Committee on Armed Services, 95 Cong. 2 sess. (GPO, 1978), pt. 4: *Manpower and Personnel,* pp. 2823–24.

enlisted personnel area . . . supervisory E-5 and E-6 skill levels were less than 50 percent of allowances."[30]

How seriously do such shortages impair the nation's defense capabilities? How great a gain in military effectiveness could be expected if these shortages were alleviated? In the absence of a comprehensive and meaningful index describing military output, it is difficult to gauge improvements in effectiveness in a quantitative sense. Nonetheless, tests undertaken by the armed services throughout the years have indicated that the link between experience and effectiveness in the defense area can be very strong. As early as 1957, the Defense Advisory Committee on Professional and Technical Compensation reported the results of tests conducted by the U.S. Navy:

An anti-submarine squadron was selectively staffed with experienced personnel throughout the squadron. . . . This unit was far more effective than similar squadrons not manned with experienced personnel. The level of aircraft availability, utilization and aircrew efficiency was outstanding. This squadron had no aircraft accidents . . . as contrasted to nine accidents resulting in complete losses suffered by other squadrons of this type during the same period.[31]

Furthermore, "in the field of radar detection, fleet evaluation shows that a destroyer equipped with standard electronic equipment and manned with personnel of excellent ability and experience has the capability of providing the same coverage as about three of the same type of ships operating in company if these latter are manned with personnel of average ability and experience."[32] According to the committee, "the effect of experience added to training can be seen in the field of guided missiles in all services. In general, missiles prepared and used by a group with a few years experience perform twice as effectively as missiles prepared by a group with similar training but no backlog of experience."[33]

More than 20 years later, similar observations were included in the *Defense Resource Management Study,* a report requested by President Carter and submitted to the secretary of defense.

A more experienced force . . . would be better able to absorb and train new personnel required to reconstitute and sustain the combat forces . . . in most NATO/Warsaw Pact scenarios. . . . Increasing the experience level in a pool of flight-line maintenance technicians could dramatically increase a squadron's rapid turnaround capability. . . . Component repair at the intermediate mainte-

30. *Congressional Record,* daily edition (April 6, 1977), p. S5698.
31. *Report of the Defense Advisory Committee on Professional and Technical Compensation,* vol. 1: *Military Personnel* (GPO, 1957), p. 28.
32. Ibid., p. 31.
33. Ibid., p. 32.

nance level requires highly skilled personnel. . . . Increases in quality of repair
. . . can dramatically reduce mean-times-between-removals because the field
reliability of components is increased. . . . An experienced component repair
force could also do more of the repair that is currently coded as depot-level.
This would increase theater self-sufficiency and decrease the inventory pipeline investment requirement [and] . . . the number of mission-ready aircraft
would increase.[34]

Current Imbalances

As suggested above, the military's preoccupation with youthfulness at
the expense of experience may not be providing the nation with the most
effective armed forces possible at current budgetary levels. Just how severe a shortage of experienced personnel the armed forces are faced with
is difficult to gauge with any precision. However, the high concentration
of technicians and craftsmen in the military, the training investment they
represent, and the importance of the defense mission indicate a need for
a level of experience higher among armed forces personnel than in the
rest of the economy. Thus one would expect the military to rely on seasoned, mature workers to an even greater extent than civilian employers
do. The mere youthfulness of military personnel suggests imbalances and
underscores the need for change. Many military jobs, particularly those
involving technical and craft skills now assigned to young inexperienced
workers, can be more effectively performed by seasoned personnel.

The staffing of comparable occupations in civilian employment indicates that civilian employers tap the experience potential of their workers
to a much greater extent than does the military. For example, table 3-4
shows that the civilian sector relies on workers over 44 years of age to a
much greater extent than the armed services do. Also evident is the extent
to which enlisted personnel in the technical jobs and particularly in the
craftsmen jobs are younger than their civilian counterparts. Only 14
percent of military enlisted personnel engaged in technical work and 12
percent of those in the craftsmen jobs are over 35 years of age; the figures
for civilian sector workers are 55 and 56 percent, respectively.

When the extreme age groups are excluded—the youngest in the military and the oldest in the civilian sector—the armed forces are still shown
to employ relatively fewer mature, experienced personnel. Table 3-5,

34. Donald B. Rice, *Defense Resource Management Study,* Final Report (GPO,
1979), pp. 66–68.

Table 3-4. Age Distribution of Military Enlisted Personnel and Civilian Sector Male Workers by Major Occupational Category, 1977
Percent

Major occupational category	Age			
	17–24[a]	*25–34*	*35–44*	*Over 44*
Military enlisted personnel[b]				
Technical workers	53	33	13	1
Clerical workers	43	36	18	2
Craftsmen	59	29	11	1
Other	64	26	10	1
Civilian sector male workers				
Technical workers[c]	10	35	23	32
Clerical workers	25	25	16	34
Craftsmen	17	27	21	35
Other[d]	40	20	13	28

Sources: Unpublished data provided by the Office of the Assistant Secretary of Defense for Manpower, Reserve Affairs, and Logistics and by the U.S. Department of Labor, Bureau of Labor Statistics. Percentages are rounded.
a. Civilian percentages include 16-year-olds.
b. Military occupational categories are defined in table 3-3, except "other," which includes "service and supply handlers" and "infantry, gun crews, and seamanship specialists" categories.
c. Includes professional occupations.
d. Nonfarm laborers and service workers.

which presents the distribution of military personnel and civilian employed males aged 25–44 by major occupational category, shows that even in unskilled jobs in the civilian sector, the proportion of workers 35–44 years of age is high. In the armed forces, however, older personnel are concentrated in the clerical occupations.

The emphasis on youthfulness not only appears unwarranted but may also be misplaced. For example—and this is significant—the proportion of enlisted personnel aged seventeen to twenty-four is the smallest in the clerical job category. Table 3-4 shows that a fifth of all enlisted clerical workers are over the age of 34. This pattern is quite unlike that prevailing in civilian employment, where clerical jobs are more likely to be staffed by young workers, as both training requirements and formal qualifications are minimal. In fact, for these reasons clerical jobs in the civilian economy serve as the lower steps on the occupational ladder, allowing for upward mobility to more skilled jobs. Yet in the armed forces clerical workers account for a surprisingly large percentage of the experienced military work force.

A related point deserves emphasis. Since civilian personnel employed by the Department of Defense are considerably older on the average than military personnel, it is commonly held that they provide some of the ex-

Table 3-5. Distribution of Experienced Military Enlisted Personnel and Civilian Sector Male Workers Aged 25 to 44 by Major Occupational Category, 1977
Percent

Major occupational category[a]	Age		
	25–29	*30–34*	*35–44*
Technical workers			
Enlisted military personnel	45	26	29
Civilian male workers[b]	30	30	40
Clerical workers			
Enlisted military personnel	40	26	33
Civilian male workers	35	26	39
Craftsmen			
Enlisted military personnel	46	26	28
Civilian male workers	29	27	44
Other			
Enlisted military personnel	47	26	27
Civilian male workers[c]	35	26	39
All occupations			
Enlisted military personnel	45	26	29
Civilian male workers	30	27	42

Sources: Unpublished data provided by the Office of the Assistant Secretary of Defense for Manpower, Reserve Affairs, and Logistics and by the U.S. Department of Labor, Bureau of Labor Statistics. Percentages are rounded.

a. Military occupational categories are defined in table 3-3, except for "other," which includes the "service and supply handlers" and "infantry, gun crews, and seamanship specialists" categories.

b. Includes professional occupations.

c. Nonfarm laborers and service workers.

pertise the military personnel lack. The occupational distribution of defense civilians, however, indicates that these mature, experienced workers are not being used to greatest advantage. Table 3-6 shows the distribution of defense civilians among the major occupational groups; each group contains federal civilian jobs equivalent to military enlisted jobs. As the table indicates, 58 percent of defense civilians are concentrated in clerical and service and supply skills, as are 56 percent of those aged 40 and above. But the participation of defense civilians in the technical occupations is extremely limited; only 4 percent work in electronic equipment repair, and slightly more, 6 percent, in other technical and allied specialties, while a negligible 2 percent work as medical and dental specialists and in communications and intelligence. This suggests that the benefits expected from the employment of a more experienced civilian complement have not been fully captured by the military establishment.

Table 3-7 presents the occupational distribution of military personnel by age and by service. The data in this table serve a two-fold purpose:

Table 3-6. Distribution of Full-Time Defense Civilian Personnel by Major Occupational Category, 1977

Major occupational category[a]	Percent of full-time defense civilians	
	All ages	40 and over
Technical workers	**12**	**12**
Electronic equipment repairmen	4	4
Communications and intelligence specialists	1	1
Medical and dental specialists	1	1
Other technical and allied specialists	6	6
Clerical workers[b]	**41**	**37**
Craftsmen	**31**	**33**
Electrical/mechanical equipment repairmen	10	11
All other craftsmen	20	22
Other[c]	**17**	**19**

Source: Unpublished data provided by the Office of the Assistant Secretary of Defense for Manpower, Reserve Affairs, and Logistics. Percentages are rounded.

a. Categories (defined in table 3-3) are the same for defense civilians as for enlisted personnel, being based on the Defense Department occupational classification system.

b. The "functional support and administration" category.

c. Includes "service and supply handlers" and a small number of civilians—mostly seamen—in the "infantry, gun crews, and seamanship" category.

first, they amplify the information in table 3-4, illustrating the contrast in job-staffing practices between the civilian sector and each of the armed services; and second, they roughly indicate the extent to which improvements are possible.

The data suggest that the Navy and the Air Force—the services with the largest concentration of technicians and craftsmen—would stand to gain the most by moving toward a more experienced work force. But improvements are also possible in the Army and the Marine Corps—the services in which the necessity for youth and vigor has been emphasized to a relatively higher degree. In fact, as the data in table 3-7 show, the Army and the Marine Corps should consider utilizing more experienced personnel in *all* occupational areas.

IN CONCLUSION, the relationship among experience, individual productivity, and military effectiveness has long been obscured. The analysis above indicates, however, that for a range of military jobs—especially those on the skilled end of the spectrum—experience is more important than physical prowess. Moreover, as a result of technological and organi-

Table 3-7. Age Distribution of Military Enlisted Personnel, by Service, and of Civilian Sector Male Workers by Major Occupational Category, 1977[a]
Percent

Major occupational category[a]	Age			
	17–24	*25–34*	*35–44*	*Over 44*
Technical workers				
Civilian sector	10	35	23	32
Army	56	32	11	1
Navy	54	33	12	1
Marine Corps	67	25	7	1
Air Force	45	35	18	2
Clerical workers				
Civilian sector	25	25	16	34
Army	47	35	16	2
Navy	42	38	18	2
Marine Corps	61	26	12	1
Air Force	37	39	22	2
Craftsmen				
Civilian sector	17	27	21	35
Army	66	25	8	1
Navy	57	30	12	1
Marine Corps	72	22	6	*
Air Force	53	33	13	1
Other[b]				
Civilian sector	40	20	13	28
Army	65	26	8	1
Navy	40	37	21	2
Marine Corps	84	13	3	*
Air Force	56	30	13	1

Source: Unpublished data provided by the Office of the Assistant Secretary of Defense for Manpower, Reserve Affairs, and Logistics and by the U.S. Department of Labor, Bureau of Labor Statistics. Percentages are rounded.
* Less than 1 percent.
a. Occupational categories are defined in table 3-3.
b. For civilian sector, includes nonfarm laborers and service workers. For military, includes "service and supply handlers" and "infantry, gun crews, and seamanship specialists" categories.

zational trends, the occupational structure of U.S. military forces has demanded more and more specialized expertise and is now dominated by technical positions. Yet the armed forces, adhering to outdated policies handed down from previous eras, continue to place a greater premium on youth and vigor at the expense of experience. The extent of the imbalance is hard to pin down, but if civilian sector practices are any indication, the potential for improvements in personnel utilization by the armed forces may indeed be considerable.

CHAPTER FOUR

IMPLICATIONS FOR RESERVE FORCES
AND MILITARY-CIVIL RELATIONS

ONE OF THE SIDE EFFECTS of staffing military jobs with more experienced personnel would be a reduction in the flow of personnel into and out of the armed forces. As indicated in chapter 2, such a prospect is bound to worry those who feel that a large turnover in the active forces is necessary to keep the reserve forces manned and those who argue that for various reasons American society benefits from processing large numbers of youths through the military system.

The Reserve Forces Problem

A reduction in turnover among personnel in the active forces would decrease the pool of trained manpower available for duty in the reserve establishment, a pool that many believe is already too small. For the most part concern has been confined to the Army components—the Army Reserve and Army National Guard—since the other services have had less difficulty keeping their reserve components up to strength.[1]

1. The magnitude of the problem is suggested in part by the Army's relative dependence on its reserve component, shown below (in thousands):

Military service	Active personnel	Reserve unit personnel	Reserve personnel as percent of total personnel
Army	774	550	42
Navy	532	87	14
Marine Corps	192	33	15
Air Force	571	146	20

(U.S. Department of Defense, Office of the Assistant Secretary of Defense for Manpower, Reserve Affairs, and Logistics, *Manpower Requirements Report for FY 1979* [DOD, 1978], pp. II-4, II-7.)

Army Reserve Mobilization Requirements

Military planners estimate that 1.78 million trained U.S. Army troops would be required within 120 days after mobilization to support a protracted conflict in Europe between the forces of the North Atlantic Treaty Organization (NATO) and the Warsaw Pact nations.[2] With but 774,000 total personnel in the active Army to start with, about 1 million additional personnel would have to be raised within four months. The reserve components ostensibly are designed to meet this need. The Ready Reserve consists of two major elements: the Selected Reserve and the Individual Ready Reserve (IRR). The former is composed almost exclusively of organized units whose members train regularly; the latter consists of individuals with prior military service who neither train nor get paid but who are liable to call-up in an emergency.[3] In fiscal year 1978 the strength of the Army Selected Reserve was about 550,000 trained personnel and that of the Individual Ready Reserve was approximately 177,000. Counting an additional 80,000 to 90,000 personnel that would be available from other sources, namely the Standby Reserve and Retired Reserve components,[4] the army could muster at most about 820,000 trained reservists, some 180,000 shy of its stated mobilization requirement.

Accordingly, the Army has taken measures to reduce the shortfalls in both the Selected Reserve and the Individual Ready Reserve. In the former case recruitment programs are being stepped up, bonuses are being offered, advertising campaigns are being mounted, attrition is being curbed, and training options are being widened.[5] Several steps have also been taken to deal with IRR problems: automatic transfers from the IRR to Standby Reserve status after completing the first five years of the six-year obligation have been terminated; persons leaving active and Selected Reserve duty are being screened for entry into the IRR; and some reserv-

2. U.S. Department of Defense, Office of the Secretary of Defense, *A Report to Congress on U.S. Conventional Reinforcements to NATO* (DOD, 1976), p. IX-3.

3. For a fuller discussion of the organization of the reserve forces, see Martin Binkin, *U.S. Reserve Forces: The Problem of the Weekend Warrior* (Brookings Institution, 1974).

4. Kenneth J. Coffey, *Manpower for Military Mobilization,* Studies in Defense Policy (American Enterprise Institute for Public Policy Research, 1978), p. 22.

5. U.S. Department of Defense, Office of the Assistant Secretary of Defense for Manpower, Reserve Affairs, and Logistics, *America's Volunteers: A Report on the All-Volunteer Armed Forces* (DOD, 1978), pp. 117–18.

ists are being permitted to remain in the IRR even though they have completed their military service obligation. Taken together these initiatives are expected to add about 70,000 people to the IRR by 1984.[6]

Additional changes are under consideration. Lengthening military service obligations and including in the mobilization pool military personnel and veterans who have satisfied their military obligations are expected to ease the problem. According to the Pentagon: "These initiatives together with those already taken should provide . . . the management flexibility needed to insure an adequate supply of pretrained assets."[7] The success of these measures, however, is not at all certain, and thus any reduction in turnover that would reduce the pool of veterans on which the reserves depend so heavily is likely to cause concern among those who view current reserve manning shortfalls as an undue risk to national security.

Before the value of more experienced active forces is discounted on these grounds, however, several questions need to be addressed. What are the assumptions underlying the Army's stated requirement for trained manpower? Are they appropriate? Are they consistent with assumptions used in the planning of other resources? Is the reserves' heavy dependence on the pool of veterans leaving active service an efficient recruitment strategy?

The Validity of Mobilization Requirements

Since so much depends on the mobilization requirement for 1.78 million trained Army personnel, it is important to examine the validity of that premise.[8] Its specific rationale flows from a set of assumptions underlying

6. Ibid., p. 124.
7. Ibid., p. 125.
8. A fundamental question raised by many observers is whether a conventional war between the forces of NATO and the Warsaw Pact would last long enough for the reserves to make any difference in the first place. Shortly after assuming the post of secretary of defense in the Ford administration, James R. Schlesinger concluded that "except under very optimistic assumptions about the time required for [Warsaw] Pact mobilization and deployment, the upshot is that the majority of Army Guard and Reserve units cannot play a role in the early and critical stages of a war in Central Europe." (See *Report of the Secretary of Defense James R. Schlesinger to the Congress on the FY 1975 Defense Budget and FY 1975–1979 Defense Program* [U.S. Department of Defense, 1974], p. 96.) As small as the probability might be that such a war might drag on, however, it is important to hedge against it. The key questions, of course, are (1) how much of a hedge is necessary, and (2) what form it should take.

war scenarios that cannot be replicated without access to classified information. Yet the validity of the requirement has been questioned openly by Kenneth J. Coffey, a Defense Department consultant and an authority on military mobilization.

The determination by the army that 1.78 million personnel would be required upon mobilization must be subject to careful scrutiny. All subsequent judgments concerning the level of shortfalls and the goals of corrective actions depend on this figure, and policy makers must be sure that all these men and women are needed. The army's estimate of replacements needed for potential casualties should also be carefully analyzed. It is possible that Pentagon planners have set manpower requirements without a careful in-depth evaluation of needs—a common practice during the manpower-rich draft years. Even worse, the scenario could have been influenced by a predetermined decision to justify large numbers of mobilized reserves, thus providing a basis for continuing the current strength and high funding levels of the reserve forces. Although there is no evidence that the estimates of manpower requirements are biased, such determinations, by necessity, contain a great number of subjective judgments made by the planners and their leaders. In addition, the determinations of requirements usually lack the support of comprehensive research.[9]

Scenario assumptions aside, the question of whether the particular functions assigned to reserve units serve a useful national security purpose in the first place need to be examined. Some reserve units, tailored for a replay of World War II, no longer appear relevant to the contingencies now envisioned.[10] The extent to which there are now such marginal units in the reserve forces structure is difficult to predict; an effort has been made over the past several years to eliminate civil affairs, public information, and other units whose irrelevance was particularly conspicuous.

The Consistency of Mobilization Requirements

The need to mobilize over 1 million reservists can be debated on other grounds as well. Could these forces be equipped? Could they be deployed within four months? Here again, the assumptions by necessity are shrouded in military secrecy, but Coffey has raised the possibilities that the Army might be unable to equip and supply many of the mobilized

9. Coffey, *Manpower for Military Mobilization*, p. 41.
10. See Binkin, *U.S. Reserve Forces*, for a discussion of this issue.

units and that the nation might lack sufficient transport capabilities to meet the deployment schedule.

If, as is likely, the current capability for airlift and sealift is inadequate, it would be futile to spend great sums of money on incentives or to draft personnel to provide additional reinforcements who could not be quickly transported to the battlefields, or who, once there, could not be supported with necessary amounts of food, ammunition, and other supplies.[11]

To the extent that other resource limitations constrain the rate at which the armed forces can deploy reinforcements, reliance on conscripts rather than on reservists becomes a feasible proposition. At some point, it can be argued, partially manned cadres capable of molding conscripts into an operational unit after mobilization starts become a cost-effective alternative to fully manned reserve units.

The issue, of course, boils down to the relative merits of raising and training civilian armies by cadres *after* mobilization or of maintaining reserve units during peacetime. The financial implications are obvious: the costs of a partially manned cadre unit would be far lower than those of a fully manned one. On the effectiveness side, however, much would depend on how rapidly the cadre, which would have to organize, equip, and train personnel after mobilization, could be deployed as a unit relative to how rapidly reserve units that are already organized could be—or would need to be—deployed.[12]

Utilization of Manpower in the Reserves

There is also the question of whether the current reserve recruitment strategy, which relies extensively on veterans leaving the active forces, is appropriate. This is important; to the extent that the Army Reserve units could rely more heavily on recruitment directly from the civilian labor force, the effects of reduced turnover in the active forces could be mitigated. A full assessment of this issue would require a more detailed analysis of the reserve establishment than is possible here, but a cursory examination of the occupational and age distributions of the Army Selected

---

11. Coffey, *Manpower for Military Mobilization*, p. 42.

12. One of the important questions concerning the mobilization problem is how soon the first draftees could be delivered to the armed forces, and the answer depends in large measure on the status of the selective service system. For a discussion of this issue, see Congressional Budget Office, *The Selective Service System: Mobilization Capabilities and Options for Improvement*, Budget Issue Paper for Fiscal Year 1980 (Government Printing Office, 1978).

Table 4-1. Distribution of Enlisted Personnel, Army Selected Reserve and Active Army, by Major Occupational Category, 1977

	Enlisted personnel (percent)	
Major occupational category[a]	*Army Selected Reserve*[b]	*Active Army*
Technical workers[c]	15	24
Clerical workers[d]	19	17
Craftsmen[e]	22	18
Other[f]	43	41
Infantry and gun crews	27	29
Total	100	100

Source: Unpublished data provided by the Office of the Assistant Secretary of Defense for Manpower, Reserve Affairs, and Logistics. Percentages are rounded.

a. Categories are based on the Department of Defense occupational classification system discussed in chapter 3.

b. Includes both Army Reserve and Army National Guard units.

c. Includes electronic equipment repairmen, communications and intelligence specialists, medical and dental specialists, and other technical and allied specialists.

d. The "functional support and administration" category.

e. Includes "electrical/mechanical equipment repairmen" and "craftsmen" categories.

f. Includes "service and supply handlers" and Army occupations included in the "infantry, gun crews, and seamanship specialists" category.

Reserve suggests that there is some room for the reserve establishment to adjust in a cost-effective manner to a reduced flow of manpower through the active forces.[13]

The occupational distribution of the 435,000 enlisted personnel in Army Reserve units in 1977 is shown in table 4-1, along with the occupational distribution of Army enlisted personnel on active duty. The data show that the reserves employ proportionately more clerks and other generally inexperienced workers than the active force does. Army Reserve forces employ relatively fewer specialists, on the other hand, than the active Army does; taken together, only 37 percent of the reservists are classified as technical workers or craftsmen, compared with 42 percent of the soldiers in the active Army.

But reservists in the enlisted force are also much older than their counterparts on active duty, as shown in the percentages below (which exclude trainees and students):

	Reservists	*Active duty personnel*
Under age 23	18	46
Over age 34	21	11

13. While this study does not include a detailed occupational analysis of the Selected Reserve establishment, it provides the tools necessary for assessing the manpower utilization policy. Consequently a straightforward application of the principles set forth in the previous chapters is possible in the case of the Army Selected Reserve.

The proportion of active personnel under the age of 23 is 2.5 times as large as the proportion of reserve members in the same age group; and the percentage of reservists over the age of 34 is almost twice as high as the percentage of active personnel in the same age group. In other words the average reservist has far more experience than his active counterpart, a not unexpected result of reliance on active-force veterans as a source of supply.

It appears, however, that the reserves are not putting this experience to the most efficient use. For example, of all enlisted personnel aged 35 and above in the Army National Guard, over 60 percent are trained in unskilled or clerical occupations, about 25 percent in craftsmen jobs, and the remaining 14 percent in the professional and technical specialties.[14] Thus as matters now stand, the Army employs a younger force than necessary to perform its regular mission and an older force than necessary for its reserve-related mission.

In view of its occupational structure, why the reserve establishment needs to depend so heavily on the active duty force as a manpower supply source is open to question. Since many clerical, service, and supply-related duties can be performed by younger people with minimal training, it would appear that the Army Reserve could rely on new enlistments for filling such jobs to a greater degree than is now the case. Thus the Army should consider increasing the proportion of recruits directly from civilian life to fill combat arms billets in its reserve components, while inducing higher retention among personnel in technical and craft jobs. On net, the Army Reserve establishment would then not have to rely as much on turnover in the active forces, and it could well experience a fall in total accession requirements.

If the occupational structure of the Army Selected Reserve reflects the skills of the personnel that can be recruited and retained rather than actual mission-related requirements, the need for reform is even greater. If the real occupational needs of the Army Reserve are largely for persons trained in combat-related tasks, then the appropriate market for recruits could well be one and the same: civilian youths. In that case policies that would reduce the Army's reliance on new accessions for the active duty force could not but have a desirable effect on the supply of enlistments to the selected reserves. Alternatively, if these occupational data understate the needs of the Army Selected Reserve for experienced specialists, then

14. Based on unpublished data provided by the Office of the Assistant Secretary of Defense for Manpower, Reserve Affairs, and Logistics.

policies that emphasize improved retention among reserve personnel deserve greater consideration.

In view of the above it is clear that there are valid reasons for concern about the future of the reserve forces. This concern, however, should center not so much on the *size* of the pool of manpower available for duty in the reserves as on the more fundamental issues of the mission and role of the reserve forces, the occupational needs deriving from that mission, and the staffing of jobs in the reserve establishment.

Military-Civil Issues

As discussed in chapter 2, some perceive that a large turnover of military manpower yields important benefits for American society: the flow of men into and out of the military establishment is thought (1) to guard against the growth of a separate military ethos, and (2) to provide otherwise unavailable training opportunities to many youths, particularly the disadvantaged. Those who hold these views would be likely to oppose measures that would diminish the flow of people into and out of the armed forces.

Ideological Balance and the Military Ethos

The relationship between the nation's armed forces and the social environment has long been a subject of controversy among social and political scientists. A relevant issue in the scholarly debate concerns the representativeness of the military establishment: to what extent would reduced turnover and, by implication, increased professionalism contribute to an ideological imbalance that would isolate the military from society? One school of thought holds that a military not broadly representative of society fosters its own rigid ethos and weakens civilian control; other scholars suggest less dire consequences.

The former subscribes to the hypothesis that a military force integrated with its host society provides an informal social network to "ensure that civilian sensibilities are incorporated within the military."[15] This, so the argument goes, can be accomplished through the presence in the military

15. Jerald G. Bachman, John D. Blair, and David R. Segal, *The All-Volunteer Force: A Study of Ideology in the Military* (University of Michigan Press, 1977), p. 16.

of "in-and-outers" who maintain their identities as civilians rather than as military professionals. As Morris Janowitz, one of the principal proponents of the integration theory, summed it up:

. . . it would be in error to overlook the fact that self-selection into the volunteer force is already recruiting men with an inclination towards conservative thinking. An in-bred force, which could hold resentments toward civilian society and could, accordingly, develop a strong and uniform conservative political ideology, would in turn influence professional judgments.[16]

This theory has been questioned on at least four counts.

First, it has been noted that "no simple link between military professionalism and military intervention in politics has to date been shown to exist."[17] Although instances can be found where highly professional armies have seized political power, these have been largely in the third world, suggesting that such action is also influenced, according to one scholar, by "the level of political culture."[18]

Others contend that even if the military's link with society is considered important, it can be maintained through means other than the representativeness of its personnel.

There is now significant interaction between the military and the rest of society. The military is not isolated from the mass media which permeate all walks of life. Also, the forces contain a wide variety of specialists, not only in air, sea and ground combat, but also in all branches of engineering and science, in computer applications, medicine and dentistry, law, aviation, personnel management, ship building, and others. These men are often in daily contact with their fellow professionals in the civilian sector. . . . The Defense Department employs more than one million civilians, and many officers serve tours of duty which require daily contact with the business community, academic institutions, and other civilian organizations.[19]

16. Morris Janowitz, "The U.S. Forces and the Zero Draft," *Adelphi Papers,* no. 94 (London: International Institute for Strategic Studies, 1973), p. 27.

17. Jacques van Doorn, "The Decline of the Mass Army in the West: General Reflections," *Armed Forces and Society,* vol. 1 (Winter 1975), p. 154. It is interesting to note that the only military takeover in Europe in the past 25 years—the Greek colonels' coup d'état of 1967—was carried out by a group of officers in "an army with the highest proportion of conscripts (88 per cent) of all NATO forces." See Erwin Häckel, "Military Manpower and Political Purpose," *Adelphi Papers,* no. 72 (London: The Institute for Strategic Studies, 1970), p. 23.

18. S. E. Finer, *The Man on Horseback: The Role of the Military in Politics* (Praeger, 1962), pp. 86–88. According to Finer, in the "mature political cultures" of such nations as the United States, Britain, Switzerland, Canada, and Australia "public sanction for [military intervention] would be unobtainable" (p. 88).

19. *The Report of the President's Commission on an All-Volunteer Armed Force* (GPO, 1970), p. 138.

Third, it has been pointed out, the preponderantly conservative officer corps has always been the dominant influence on military values. According to one observer, "It is always this elite, and not the rank and file, which makes decisions about political action and social pressure."[20] And there is little evidence to indicate that the views of the latter carry much weight with the former.

Finally, at the extreme some argue that whether military forces are representative of, or closely integrated with, the broader civilian society has little bearing on the issue of civilian control. In fact, proponents of "objective civilian control" advocate "autonomous military professionalism"; civilian control exercised through a formal chain of command "achieves its end by militarizing the military, making them the tool of the state," as opposed to the integration approach, which "achieves its end by civilianizing the military, making them the mirror of the state."[21] The benefits of the "objective" approach, according to Samuel P. Huntington, its principal proponent, are that it "produces the lowest possible level of military political power with respect to all civilian groups," while preserving "that essential element of power which is necessary for the existence of a military profession."[22]

While the issue remains far from settled, the historical record holds little to suggest that more professionalized U.S. armed forces would pose a risk to civilian control of the military establishment.

Social Benefits of Military Training

Some also contend that high turnover among military personnel is desirable insofar as it allows a large number of youths to take advantage of the training opportunities the services offer; once exposed to such training, youths become more employable and hence can have better options in their civilian working life.

Emphasis on the social benefits of military training was especially strong in the mid-1960s under the Johnson administration. Apparently administration planners believed that the services had excess training capacity, and in a desire to emphasize the potential contribution of the mili-

20. van Doorn, "The Decline of the Mass Army," p. 155.
21. Samuel P. Huntington, *The Soldier and the State: The Theory and Politics of Civil-Military Relations* (Belknap Press of Harvard University Press, 1957), p. 83.
22. Ibid., p. 84.

tary in the war against poverty, they set out to upgrade the skills of youth. Defense Secretary Robert McNamara's Project One Hundred Thousand, a plan committing the military to accept 100,000 special enlistments a year, was intended to open military training opportunities to the nation's disadvantaged youths. To this end some aptitude test standards were waived for inductees without a high school degree, and enlistment standards were lowered. As a result, the need for remedial procedures arose, and modifications in the training curricula had to be made.

Later, Project Transition committed the services to improving the transferability of military training to the civilian sector:

By the fall of 1967, a number of pilot programs had already been established at military bases under which enlisted personnel nearing the end of their tours of duty were offered the opportunity to enter into selected vocational training courses or educational upgrading programs designed specifically to help them increase their employability, after leaving military service.[23]

Whether transferability of training has improved a little or a lot as a result of these programs, few would doubt that the participants have reaped some benefits. These benefits, however, were not—and could not be—conferred at zero cost.

Three issues may therefore be raised in connection with the social benefits of military training.

First, the armed services manpower budget does not provide funds for general purpose training; rather, the cost of training is borne by the military explicitly for the purpose of preparing men and women to fill productive positions. These costs depend on the rates at which trainees fail to fill such positions: the higher the attrition rates, the higher the costs. As a result, policies that emphasize military training opportunities for their benefits to society should be judged also in terms of their potential costs to the taxpaying public.[24] This would call for a comprehensive assessment of the social value of the benefits of military training.

In this connection the larger issue of the potential role of the military as a training institution for civilians may be raised. Not by accident, the education and training of youths has traditionally been the mission of

23. Harold Wool, *The Military Specialist: Skilled Manpower for the Armed Forces* (Johns Hopkins Press, 1968), p. 183.

24. When the draft was in effect, pay for conscripts was exceedingly low; thus the variable component of the training costs was a smaller proportion of the total than is the case today. It is not surprising that because the costs were kept at artificially low levels in the 1960s, the administration had no clear disincentives not to promote the social role of the military as a training institution.

civilian institutions, but the role of the federal government in this enterprise has expanded considerably, especially since the 1960s. The 1979 federal budget calls for expenditures of $14.4 billion on postsecondary education programs, as payments to students and to civilian institutions.[25] Budgeted outlays in 1979 for federal programs specifically providing on-the-job and institutional training, work experience, and public service employment to youths under the Comprehensive Employment and Training Act were over $11 billion;[26] many of these programs are intended to serve low-income, disadvantaged, hard-to-employ youths. In view of the scope and the cost of these programs, it is not clear why the armed forces should assume general training responsibilities. It is even less clear why reductions in military accessions requirements (which would occur if turnover among enlisted personnel fell) should give rise to any concerns other than those relating to the effectiveness of the armed forces.

Second, it may be argued that an expanded role for the military in domestic programs would distort the socioeconomic composition of the armed forces. Should the provision of training opportunities become more than incidental in nature, the armed forces would have to accept a larger number of beneficiaries—principally poor, black, disadvantaged youths. Some observers consider even the present composition to be undesirable and feel that with the elimination of the draft, the armed forces have ceased to be representative of American society and now attract a larger proportion of the poor, the blacks, and the disadvantaged. According to a *New York Times* editorial, May 13, 1978:

With the sons of the middle classes deferred for college, Vietnam became a poor man's war, with disproportionate numbers of blacks serving in the combat forces. Recruit pay was quadrupled to increase volunteers and, finally, the draft was ended, but the imbalance was only accentuated. There are more poor in the Army now, not less. The percentage of blacks among Army enlisted men in 1971 was 13 percent, about the same as in the nation; it is now double that among Army recruits. . . . Both white and black recruits come in good part from the unemployed 17 percent of the nation's young—and the 34 percent jobless among minorities.

Third, an expanded role for the military in social programs may have adverse implications for force effectiveness. If the primary mission of the

25. David W. Breneman, "Education," in Joseph A. Pechman, ed., *Setting National Priorities: The 1979 Budget* (Brookings Institution, 1978), table 4-4, pp. 112–13.

26. John L. Palmer, "Employment and Income Security," ibid., tables 3-4 and 3-5, pp. 77–80.

military is the maintenance of an adequate defense posture at a given budget, then diverting resources away from uses relating to that mission would undermine force effectiveness: "To maximize such [training] spillovers, would call for a healthy investment in training and, as far as practical, low entry standards. This does not match the military's desire to avoid the problems of dealing with deficiently educated and poorly prepared workers and the desire to secure the highest quality workers possible is understandable."[27]

In view of the above, it is not clear that reduced turnover in the enlisted force would have—or need have—adverse implications for the role of the armed forces in society. This role has by and large been incidental to the main mission of the military, usually an unintended consequence of it.

THIS CHAPTER puts into perspective the concerns of those who view a reduction in personnel turnover in the active military forces as a threat to the viability of the reserve forces or as counterproductive to certain social purposes. First, whether the reserve forces as now constituted serve a relevant national security purpose is open to question; even if they are considered relevant, the evidence suggests that they could continue to fulfill their mission while reducing their reliance on the turnover of personnel in the active forces. Second, whether or not a more experienced and hence more professional military force would jeopardize civilian control of the military is a subject of scholarly disagreement; at any rate, the negative consequences have not been demonstrated so strongly that the implications of increased turnover for civilian control should be viewed as a constraint. Finally, the vocational training benefits that are associated with high turnover are largely incidental to the military mission. This is not to say that these considerations should be ignored, but rather that they should not be given undue emphasis in determining the appropriate experience mix of military personnel in the active forces.

27. Sar A. Levitan and Karen Cleary Alderman, *Warriors at Work: The Volunteer Armed Force,* Sage Library of Social Research, 58 (Sage Publications, 1977), p. 41.

CHAPTER FIVE

YOUTH, EXPERIENCE, AND COST

THE VIEW THAT experienced people are somehow too costly for the armed forces is implicit in the military's accent on youth. In part this view of manpower cost relationships in the defense area may be traced directly to the "youth and vigor" doctrine—why incur higher costs for less desirable (that is, older) workers?

Undoubtedly contributing to this viewpoint are the difficulties involved in assessing the effect on military capability of changes in the experience mix. But even those who concede that experienced workers may be more valuable to the armed forces are concerned that the budgetary costs of a richer experience mix would perhaps exceed the value of the contribution of the more mature workers to national security.[1] Several factors give rise to this concern: (1) experienced personnel command a higher level of compensation than do those with less experience; (2) the cost of military retirement is imposed disproportionately by experienced personnel since they are more likely to become eligible for retirement annuities; (3) extra financial incentives are needed to induce many to remain in the armed forces beyond the initial enlistment period; and (4) older persons have more dependents on the average than their younger colleagues do, thus giving rise to higher medical, housing, travel, and other dependent-related costs.

1. In a statement to the Department of Defense Subcommittee of the House Committee on Appropriations, Assistant Secretary of Defense John P. White noted: "Experienced people are more productive and are critical to the proper operation and maintenance of an increasingly complex military force. On the other hand, experienced people are paid more and are more likely to earn retirement pay." (*Department of Defense Appropriations for 1979,* Hearings before a Subcommittee of the House Committee on Appropriations, 95 Cong. 2 sess. [Government Printing Office, 1978], pt. 3: *Manpower Overview. . .,* p. 12.)

Experience and the Personnel Pipeline

In such an assessment, however, the offsetting savings made possible by a more senior force are usually ignored. The savings are realized because an older force implies not only fewer people on the military payroll (assuming a fixed number of trained workers) but lower expenditures for recruiting, outfitting, training, and moving personnel as well.

Why is this so? The answer lies in the very nature of the "closed" personnel system of the military. In an "open" organization—which most civilian organizations are—the experience level can be increased relatively quickly merely by hiring enough seasoned workers. The experience level of military personnel, however, cannot be increased by an inflow of older workers (virtually impossible in a closed system) but only by a reduced outflow of experienced personnel; if fewer experienced workers leave the system, there is less need for replacements, which the armed forces "produce" internally, and hence less reliance on their primary source—annual accessions. It is even more significant that an increase in retention among trained military personnel produces a proportionately larger decrease in the number of recruits required. This happens because of attrition: since some fraction of trainees "wash out," more than one volunteer must be recruited to offset the loss of one trained jobholder. It follows, therefore, that more than one new accession could be avoided for each trained worker that remained in the armed forces.[2]

2. In addition to this quantitative substitution (fewer people need to be trained if more people are retained) is the potential qualitative substitution: because experienced workers are more productive, it is possible that jobs can be done with fewer but more effective personnel. Focusing on qualitative substitutions may be difficult because of a one-to-one correspondence between people and jobs in the more technical occupational areas in general, and particularly in the armed forces; presumably it is the number of airplanes that determines the number of pilots (experienced or not) and not the other way around, at least in the short run. An estimate of potential qualitative substitution is found in Richard V. L. Cooper, *Military Manpower and the All-Volunteer Force,* prepared for the Defense Advanced Research Projects Agency, ARPA 189-1, R-1450 (Rand Corporation, September 1977), chap. 13. While providing a useful perspective, this approach requires a meaningful and comprehensive productivity measurement of the alternative input mixes. To date, there has been little agreement on how to measure productivity in a military setting. Because of the conceptual problems associated with the use of such indices, qualitative substitution is not considered here. Rather, the number of military jobs to be filled is held constant, and on the basis of the analysis presented in chapter 3 the potential of staffing these jobs with more experienced workers is examined.

This would result in a reduction in the total number of people on the military payroll. Of course, an increase in retention could also be used to produce a higher total strength; this would come about if accessions were held constant. It is important to note, however, that this analysis is based, not on the assumption of a fixed level of accessions, but rather on the assumption of a fixed number of trained jobholders, in which case a higher level of retention reduces the total number of people on the defense payroll.

Past efforts to quantify the relationship between accessions and retention have met with difficulties in identifying and measuring the respective costs and in analyzing the interaction between variations in the experience mix of the force and variations in the size of the pipeline. A better understanding of the issues involved can be gained with the aid of table 5-1, which presents the distribution of the enlisted force by grade and type of position at the end of fiscal year 1977. Of a total of 1.8 million enlisted personnel in the armed forces, 14 percent filled "pipeline" positions, mostly as students and trainees.[3] The remaining 86 percent were actually engaged in the production of defense services; according to the Defense Department, they fill "structure spaces." Thus the armed forces employed an average of one nonproductive person for every six productive workers.

It is undoubtedly appropriate to consider the pipeline a necessity in an organization faced with an internal supply of workers. Clearly, as long as people quit, retire, or otherwise leave the organization, new entrants are required to replace them.[4] And as long as newcomers must be processed, instructed, and trained, the pipeline is active.[5] Consequently the

3. The Department of Defense classifies pipeline positions in a single occupational area. Besides students and trainees (filling 70 percent of pipeline positions) the classification includes transients, or those traveling between assignments (about 25 percent); patients and prisoners (5 percent), and a small number of officer candidates. (Based on U.S. Department of Defense, Office of the Assistant Secretary of Defense for Manpower, Reserve Affairs, and Logistics, *Manpower Requirements Report for FY 1979* [DOD, 1978], p. VIII-2.)

4. Replacement of personnel losses in the military is, of course, possible in a quantitative sense only; qualitatively, losses are by definition superior to gains, since the latter are usually untrained.

5. Although civilian employers may also choose to train workers, they can resort to lateral transfer to replace quits both quantitatively and qualitatively. As a result, the size as well as the cost of a private firm's pipeline may be easily adjusted to meet cost-effectiveness conditions. While the armed forces could conceivably also resort to lateral transfer of workers from the civilian sector, institutional constraints discourage this option. Lateral transfer as a means to improve the experience mix of the armed forces, however, warrants further study.

Table 5-1. Distribution of Enlisted Personnel by Grade and Type of Position, September 30, 1977

| | Type of position | | | | |
| | Pipeline[a] | | Structure[b] | | Total enlisted |
Grade	Number	Percent	Number	Percent	personnel
E-1	140,939	79	36,759	21	177,698
E-2	65,949	33	136,330	67	202,279
E-3	43,048	14	273,424	86	316,472
E-4	3,595	1	397,481	99	401,076
E-5	2,213	1	315,709	99	317,922
E-6	414	*	203,886	100	204,300
E-7	161	*	117,732	100	117,893
E-8	16	*	33,864	100	33,880
E-9	2	*	13,135	100	13,137
Total	256,337	14	1,528,320	86	1,784,657

Source: Unpublished data provided by the Office of the Assistant Secretary of Defense for Manpower, Reserve Affairs, and Logistics.
* Less than 0.5 percent.
a. Mainly students and trainees, plus officer candidates, transients (those traveling between assignments), patients, and prisoners.
b. Trained persons who are actually engaged in the production of national defense services.

armed forces must incur advertising and recruitment costs in order to attract new enlistments. Second, the services must place and keep on the payroll all new enlistees, even though the latter will be unproductive for the duration of their training—that is, while in the pipeline. Third, both direct and indirect training costs must be incurred for students and trainees to achieve an even partially productive status. And fourth, additional support costs arise as a result of expanded base operations (ranging from food and shelter to recreation services).[6] Hence, even though about 98 percent of the nonproductive personnel are concentrated in the lower grades (E-1 through E-3), a substantial portion of the defense budget is absorbed by the pipeline. In fiscal year 1978, out of an estimated total budget of about $29 billion for the enlisted force, the armed services incurred some $3 billion in pipeline costs. Thus with 14 percent of the enlisted personnel in a nonproductive status, the services diverted about 10 percent of their manpower budget away from the production of current output.[7]

6. For a detailed discussion of the direct and indirect personnel costs in the military, as well as estimates of the dollar values of these costs by grade, see Martin Binkin with Herschel Kanter and Rolf H. Clark, *Shaping the Defense Civilian Work Force: Economics, Politics, and National Security* (Brookings Institution, 1978).

7. Estimates derived from unpublished data provided by the Department of Defense. Pipeline costs include training costs, travel costs, and the costs of extra

Growing Costs of the Personnel Pipeline

The growth in the costs associated with the personnel pipeline is a relatively recent phenomenon. Increases in the rate of first-term attrition,
changes in the level of military compensation and in the corresponding
characteristics of recruits, and increases in the costs of training—imposed
by the demands of increasingly sophisticated technology—have contributed to this result.

Pipeline Attrition

In recent years an increasing proportion of recruits have failed to complete their initial enlistment period. For example, because of a combination of more liberal early-release policies on the one hand and stricter dis-
charge policies on the other, male volunteers who enlisted for three or
more years of duty are leaving the service before completing their first
enlistment at a rate half again as high as that prevailing just before the
draft was abolished. Table 5-2 shows that 37 percent of the men who
volunteered in fiscal year 1974 left before completing their three years of
service, compared with only 26 percent in the fiscal 1971 cohort. Although subsequent enlistment cohorts have not yet had an opportunity to
serve for three full years, the Pentagon projects improvement, as shown in
the table.

This increase in the rate of first-term attrition means that today the
services must recruit more volunteers for each position to be filled than
they did previously. For example, the rates of attrition occurring among
the members of the fiscal 1974 cohort imply that each new recruit enlist-
ing for a three-year period could be expected to provide 1.65 productive
years of service compared with 1.92 years for the 1971 cohort. Said another way: on the basis of the most recent attrition data, the services must
now put 17 percent more recruits into the pipeline than they did in 1971
to yield the same number of productive man-years during a three-year

---

billets needed to offset work time lost due to travel or hospitalization. In addition
to these budgetary costs, there are the less obvious but just as real costs of work
forgone, as implied by the existence of the pipeline. These costs are not directly
quantifiable, since defense services are not marketed. Although it might be possible
to impute a value to defense output forgone, such an imputation is not attempted
in this study.

Table 5-2. Percentage of Male Enlisted Personnel Not Completing Three Years of Service, Selected Fiscal-Year Cohorts, by Service[a]

	Cohort (percent)			
Service	1971	1974	1977 (estimated)	1979 (projected)
Army	26	38	30	31
Navy	28	38	38	28
Marine Corps	31	37	34	30
Air Force	21	31	28	25
Department of Defense total	26	37	35	28

Source: U.S. Department of Defense, Office of the Assistant Secretary of Defense for Manpower, Reserve Affairs, and Logistics, *America's Volunteers: A Report on the All-Volunteer Armed Forces* (DOD, 1978), table 3-7, p. 65
a. Includes males who enlisted for three or more years.

enlistment period.[8] The upshot is that the cost of maintaining a pipeline of nonproductive manpower has risen significantly.

Pay Levels

The decision in 1971 to phase out conscription put the armed forces in the unfamiliar position of competing for labor in the marketplace. To enable the services to meet the competition, the Military Selective Service Act was amended in 1971. Pay increases under that legislation went predominantly to enlisted men—those just entering the service and others in the lower grades. Military pay in these categories, which had been disproportionately low, was increased by roughly 60 percent. Pay in other categories was increased by much less, averaging just 2 percent overall.

The effects were dramatic, as illustrated below in the comparison between the pay rates in effect in October 1971 and in October 1978:

		Basic pay (dollars)		Pay index (E-1 = 100)	
Grade	Years of service	October 1971	October 1978	October 1971	October 1978
E-7	Over 18	7,729	12,002	448	240
E-5	Over 4	4,806	7,506	279	150
E-1	2 or less	1,724	5,003	100	100

Whereas under conscription the armed forces could pay four and one-half inexperienced E-1s for the price of one experienced E-7, under today's pay scales that ratio drops to 2.4:1.

8. U.S. Department of Defense, Office of the Assistant Secretary of Defense for Manpower, Reserve Affairs, and Logistics, *America's Volunteers: A Report on the All-Volunteer Armed Forces* (DOD, 1978), pp. 65–66.

Recruitment Costs

As a further consequence of moving to a voluntary system, military recruitment costs have increased. Under conscription the cost associated with the procurement of recruits was largely confined to the operation of the Selective Service System. When the draft ended, the services provided enlistment bonuses to attract volunteers into combat-related and certain other technical skills. In addition each service has established elaborate recruiting operations backed up with extensive advertising campaigns. All told, it has been estimated that the incremental costs of these programs have amounted to about $1.4 billion (net of decreases in the Selective Service System) through fiscal year 1977.[9] Not including bonuses, the marginal cost of recruiting male high school graduates capable of scoring average or above on standardized entrance tests has been estimated to range from $870 a recruit for the Air Force to $3,700 a recruit for the Army in fiscal year 1977.[10]

Dependent-Related Costs

Also bearing on the issue is the recent increase in the number of young, married military personnel. In earlier eras the dependent population was confined principally to a small elitist group of officers' wives and their children; for the most part, the rank and file were unmarried and without dependents. It was not until after World War II that the military family became an institution within the enlisted ranks, officially recognized through the establishment of a full range of service for dependents: housing, on-post education, medical care, and social welfare assistance.[11] Even then, however, few young, lower-grade enlisted people were married, largely because single men bore the brunt of conscription. In 1955, for example, about 7 percent of those who entered the Army as enlisted men were already married; at that time, only 38 percent of all military personnel had a family.

9. *Additional Cost of the All-Volunteer Force,* Report to the Congress by the Comptroller General of the United States (U.S. General Accounting Office, 1978), p. 6.

10. U.S. Department of Defense, Office of the Assistant Secretary of Defense for Manpower, Reserve Affairs, and Logistics, *Use of Women in the Military,* Background Study (DOD, May 1977), p. 24. The marginal cost of recruiting other (lower-quality) males was estimated to be $150.

11. See Roger W. Little, "The Military Family," in Roger W. Little, ed., *Handbook of Military Institutions,* prepared by Inter-University Seminar on Armed Forces and Society (Sage Publications, 1971), p. 248.

By 1978 the overall proportion had reached 55 percent, partly because of an increase in the proportion of married recruits. For example, of those who entered the Army in fiscal 1978, about 10 percent were already married. Moreover, many of the volunteers who enter the service as single persons soon marry; in 1978 close to half of all enlisted men serving in their fourth year were married.

The budgetary implications are difficult to measure precisely. The most obvious differences are associated with housing allowances; for example, when entitled to the allowance, a married E-4 receives an amount about 50 percent more than an E-4 who is without dependents. Also significant are the costs incurred in providing medical care for dependents of military personnel; the cost to the government of providing health services has been estimated to be roughly $360 per dependent per year.[12]

And finally travel costs incurred when a person with a family is reassigned are also more than the cost of moving his single counterpart. The variation is due mainly to differences in the weight of household goods, which are shipped at government expense. In fiscal year 1978, for example, the difference between moving a single Army soldier and one who was married amounted to some $1,750 for an average move.[13]

Training Costs

One of the by-products of the advanced technology applied to military weapon systems has been the development of large, complex, and expensive training programs. In its fiscal 1979 budget the Department of Defense requested $5.9 billion to operate its training establishment.

Virtually all new entrants undergo basic military training; 96 percent of Army recruits then advance to an initial skill-training course, and the remaining 4 percent proceed directly to a duty assignment, either because they had previously acquired a skill in civilian life or because they can obtain the necessary skills through on-the-job training. The other services employ somewhat different training patterns. The Navy and the Marine Corps send about 70 percent of their boot camp graduates to initial skill training, and the Air Force sends 91 percent.

---

12. Estimate in *Department of Defense Appropriation Bill, 1976,* S. Rept. 446, 94 Cong. 1 sess. (GPO, 1975), p. 20, has been updated on the basis of the medical care component of the consumer price index to account for the effects of inflation.

13. Derived from U.S. Department of the Army, "Fiscal Year 1978 Permanent Change of Station Travel," January 22, 1979.

Initial skill training is offered in 880 separate courses; the average length of these courses ranges from eleven weeks in the Navy to eighteen weeks for Air Force personnel. In addition, some students continue into advanced skill training where they enter one of some 3,000 separate courses, averaging in duration from 6 weeks in the Air Force to 15 weeks in the Army. One way to measure the total training effort is in terms of "average student load," which is projected to be about 192,000 in 1979. This means that on an average day, about 192,000 persons (or one of every 11 in the armed forces) will be undergoing some form of individual (as opposed to unit) training.

In the absence of reliable historical data, it is difficult to trace with precision the effects of technological advances on the cost of training. Certainly few would dispute the contention that the typical serviceman requires more training today than did his counterpart of an earlier era. Added to that, the disproportionate increases in the pay of personnel most likely to be in a training status has reinforced the upward pressure on training costs. What can be said with certainty is that the cost of training, which is based largely on course duration, is greater for high-skill occupations. This is illustrated by the variation in the duration of some training courses designed to provide the recruit with a beginning skill:[14]

Service and course	Length of course (days)
Army	
Light weapons infantryman	56
Nuclear power plant operator	365
Navy	
Apprentice training (seaman, fireman, etc.)	16
Basic enlisted submarine training	45
Marine Corps	
Infantry training	44
Basic electronics	122
Air Force	
Security specialist	37
Avionics aerospace ground equipment	354

Thus the armed forces make a far greater investment in some personnel than in others, an issue already touched on in chapter 3 and one with important implications for the economics of retention, as will be seen later.

14. U.S. Department of Defense, Office of the Assistant Secretary of Defense for Manpower and Reserve Affairs, *Military Manpower Training Report for FY 1978: and Report on Efficiency and Effectiveness of Military Training* (DOD, 1977), p. V-5.

The Trade-Off: Gain or Retain

The growth in the costs of acquiring volunteers and of producing trained military personnel brings into question the expediency of current policies that emphasize the gain of youthful recruits rather than the retention of seasoned veterans. Does the view, long and widely held, that more experienced armed forces can be acquired only through an increase in the military payroll still stand up to scrutiny? Much depends on how the costs of placing reliance on the pipeline stack up against the costs of an alternative personnel supply source: retention. This calculation is made in table 5-3, where estimates of both the cost of replacing a typical military enlisted jobholder (grade E-4) and the cost of retaining him for an additional year are compared.

Replacement Costs

As the figures show, the cost of recruiting, processing, outfitting, training, and moving to a first job assignment a new entrant into the military labor force is about $8,260. To obtain total replacement costs, however, account must be taken of the fact that more than one recruit must enter the pipeline to offset the loss of an experienced military worker. This happens because some people drop out of the pipeline. If one uses fiscal 1977 experience as a guide, the military services recruit an average of 130 new volunteers to offset the loss of each 100 experienced workers.[15] Of these new 130, about 10 have prior military service and generally require little additional training; the remaining 120 enter the pipeline. Thus for every 10 job vacancies there are 13 accessions, 12 of whom enter the pipeline. The total cost of replacing a typical enlisted worker at the E-4 level, then, is estimated to be $9,910 ($8,260 × 1.2).

Retention Costs

Alternatively, should the vacancy not occur, these replacement costs would be avoided. In that case other costs would be incurred since the position would now be staffed by a more experienced person.

15. In fiscal year 1977 about 411,000 men and women entered the armed forces to replace about 407,500 losses, 317,000 of whom had been trained and ostensibly were filling jobs at the time of their departure.

Table 5-3. Comparison of First-Year Costs of Retaining or Replacing a Typical Military Jobholder (Grade E-4)

Fiscal year 1978 dollars

Item	Cost
Total replacement cost (subtotal $\times$ 1.2)[a]	**9,910**
Recruiting[b]	1,580
Processing[c]	1,070
Payroll[d]	3,530
Training support[e]	2,080
Subtotal (pipeline cost)	8,260
Total retention cost (not including inducements)	**2,050**
Longevity pay[f]	830
Retirement accrual[g]	850
Support[h]	370
Difference (available for retention inducements)	**7,860**

Source: Authors' estimates based on assumptions given in notes below. Except where noted otherwise, replacement cost estimates are derived from unpublished fiscal year 1977 data made available by the Office of the Assistant Secretary of Defense for Manpower, Reserve Affairs, and Logistics, adjusted for inflation.

a. Accounts for the fact that 1.2 recruits enter the pipeline to offset the loss of one jobholder.

b. Estimated recruitment and advertising costs incurred in attracting the typical volunteer.

c. Includes administrative processing, initial clothing issue, and travel costs.

d. Includes basic pay and allowances ($3,180), tax advantage ($200), and the government's implicit contribution to military retirement ($150) and assumes that the typical recruit spends six months in pipeline status. The tax advantage accrues because housing and subsistence allowances, whether in cash or in kind, are not subject to federal income tax. It is equivalent to the additional cash that would have to be provided to ensure the same take-home pay if allowances were subject to tax. The tax advantage estimate used here is based on data in *Report of the President's Commission on Military Compensation* (GPO, 1978), p. 17. The retirement cost is the amount that would have to be set aside for those in the pipeline to pay off their eventual retirement if the military retirement system were funded. Assumes that based on recent retention experience, about 8 of every 100 people who enter the pipeline will eventually qualify for retirement benefits. Under the same economic assumptions used by the administration to calculate the full cost of federal retirement systems—2.5 percent real rate of interest and 1.5 percent real wage growth—the implicit contribution toward military retirement amounts to 75 percent of the basic pay of those who eventually retire. See Richard V. L. Cooper, *Imputing the Economic Cost of Military Retirement*, prepared for the U.S. Department of Defense, Defense Advanced Research Projects Agency, Office of the Assistant Secretary of Defense for Manpower and Reserve Affairs, ARPA 189-1 (Rand Corporation, October 1975), p. 121.

e. For recruit and initial skill training, includes the cost of instructors, staff support, and expendable supplies (such as ammunition). This figure understates the full training cost; because of data limitations, expenses related to advanced skill-training courses are excluded. For the same reason, the costs associated with advanced training have also been excluded in the calculation of retention costs. These costs tend to offset one another.

f. Assumes that upon reenlistment the E-4, by virtue of entering his fifth year of service, will become qualified for a longevity step increase and that for each E-4 who reenlists, one E-3 whose promotion to E-4 would be delayed for lack of a vacancy would enter his third year of service and receive the appropriate longevity step increase.

g. Increase in the implicit retirement contribution reflects the greater propensity of senior personnel to attain retirement eligibility and the higher pay upon which the calculations are based. Entering the fifth year of service increases the probability that the E-4 will eventually retire, from 17.7 percent to 31.3 percent. Estimate also takes into account that the probability that the more senior E-3, who will enter the third year of service, will eventually retire increases from 7.5 to 8.9 percent. (Derived from unpublished continuation rates based on fiscal year 1977 experience made available by the Office of the Assistant Secretary of Defense for Manpower, Reserve Affairs, and Logistics.)

h. Increase in support costs reflects the larger dependent-related medical care and travel costs imposed by more senior personnel. The probability that an E-4 entering the fifth year of service will be married increases from 45.9 percent to 61.9, and the average number of dependents will increase from 0.75 to 1.18. The probability that an E-3 entering the third year of service will be married increases from 0.21 to 0.31, and the average number of dependents will increase from 0.30 to 0.47. (Based on unpublished data provided by the Office of the Assistant Secretary of Defense for Manpower, Reserve Affairs, and Logistics.)

Longevity pay. First, military pay rates are based on longevity as well as on grade. Increases based on longevity ("fogies" in military parlance) are generally granted at two-year intervals, with the maximum number of such step increases varying by pay grade. The size of the increase varies by step. For example, the basic pay of an E-4 jumps by 7.8 percent upon completion of four years of service and by 4 percent two years later; for an E-6, the basic pay increase is 3.7 percent at the eight-year point and 5.2 percent at the twelve-year point. Therefore to the extent that an increase in retention of trained personnel yields an inventory with a greater average number of years of service, the longevity pay component of the military payroll will be larger.

Retired pay. Higher retention rates would also be likely to result in larger retirement costs since the probability that a person will attain retirement eligibility increases with the number of years served. Based on recent experience, of every 100 persons who enter their fifth year of military service, 31 can be expected eventually to qualify for retirement benefits; of every 100 who enter their ninth year, 58 will eventually retire, and so on.

Calculating the incremental retirement costs associated with an increase in retention poses some difficult problems. The military retirement system is noncontributory and unfunded; annuities are not normally vested until members have served at least 20 years on active duty. Yet it is reasonable to allocate some portion of the eventual retirement benefit to each year of service as it is rendered. The anticipated cost can be spread over active-duty lifetime in many ways. The approach taken here is to calculate a fixed percentage of basic pay for those persons who can be expected eventually to become eligible for retirement benefits; this percentage, if set aside annually in an interest bearing fund, would accrue at a rate ensuring that the accumulated principal and interest would pay off the future benefits as they became due. If an annual real wage increase of 1.5 percent and a 2.5 percent real return on the investment funds are assumed, the percentage of base pay is about 75 percent.[16] Said another way, if the military retirement system were fully funded, an amount equivalent

16. These economic assumptions are currently employed by the administration to calculate the full cost of federal retirement programs. The implicit contribution to military retirement that would be necessary under these economic assumptions was obtained from Richard V. L. Cooper, *Imputing the Cost of Military Retirement,* prepared for the U.S. Department of Defense, Defense Advanced Research Projects Agency, Office of the Assistant Secretary of Defense for Manpower and Reserve Affairs, ARPA 189-1 (Rand Corporation, 1975), p. 121.

to 75 percent of basic pay would have to be set aside annually for each person who was expected to retire eventually.

Dependent-related support costs. A more senior force can also be expected to result in larger transportation and medical care costs, since both are related to the dependency status of the military employee. The probability that an enlisted person is married and the average number of dependents increases with the number of years served as follows:[17]

Year of service	Percent married	Average number of dependents
1	11.2	0.17
2	20.7	0.30
3	31.4	0.47
4	45.9	0.75
5	61.9	1.18
6	71.4	1.48
7	78.9	1.77
8	82.2	1.97
9	83.8	2.14
10	86.3	2.31
11	88.3	2.47
12	88.7	2.59
13	89.3	2.70
14	89.1	2.76
15	89.6	2.87
16	90.2	2.99
17	90.5	3.10
18	91.2	3.19
19	91.4	3.26
20	91.4	3.31

Inducements. It is also necessary to take into account the prospect that as additional workers are retained, additional financial inducements would be required. The services currently use reenlistment bonuses for this purpose: about 25,400 of some 55,000 military personnel who reenlisted for a second term of service in fiscal year 1978 received first installment bonuses totaling about $35 million, or an average of about $1,380 for each.[18] The number and amount of additional bonuses that

17. Based on unpublished data made available by the Office of the Assistant Secretary of Defense for Manpower, Reserve Affairs, and Logistics.

18. Data provided by Office of the Assistant Secretary of Defense for Manpower, Reserve Affairs, and Logistics. As matters now stand, selective reenlistment bonuses are given to those who reenlist within their first 10 years of service in certain military specialties. The size of each bonus depends on the reenlistee's basic pay, the number of years of additional obligated service, and his specialty and cannot ex-

would be needed to induce additional experienced workers to remain in the armed forces would depend on the degree of improvement in reenlistment rates being sought.

As table 5-3 shows, the effect on longevity pay, retirement accrual, and support costs of having a more senior worker would not be large, amounting to about $2,050. This means that the armed forces in effect could afford to pay up to $7,860 to induce the E-4 in question to remain for an additional year.[19] Payment of this amount would allow the armed forces to just break even in dollar terms—one reenlistment, 1.2 fewer replacements into the pipeline, same number of trained persons, and no change in the costs. But in terms of effectiveness, the armed forces would stand to gain by having a more experienced worker on the job.

Long-Term Effects

Thus far consideration has been given to first-year effects. In fact, as matters stand, military personnel reenlist for a period of longer than one year—generally from three to six years but typically for four years. Moreover, many of those who reenlist for a second term remain in the armed forces until attaining retirement eligibility. It is therefore important to consider the longer-term implications of the increase in the reenlistment rate considered in the illustration above.

What would be the net budgetary effect if the reenlistee, as would be expected, remained in the armed forces beyond one additional year? An estimate is provided in table 5-4, which assumes that the E-4 who reenlists after the fourth year of service will remain in the armed forces from year to year with the same probability as his recent predecessors. It is also assumed that financial inducements to retain the trained worker would be paid during the first reenlistment period at a rate that would result in a

ceed $12,000 except for bonuses reaching as much as $15,000 that are paid to certain nuclear-trained and qualified enlisted members of the naval service. See U.S. Department of Defense Instruction 1304.22, "Administration of Enlisted Personnel Bonus and Proficiency Pay Programs" (October 1, 1978).

19. At present, reenlistees receiving bonuses at the end of their first term of service are paid, on the average, $1,380 a year for a second four-year term. (Based on data provided by the Office of the Assistant Secretary of Defense for Manpower, Reserve Affairs, and Logistics.) The increase in the level of bonuses to $8,230 shown here can be viewed as the increase in the marginal cost associated with a greater number of reenlistees. An estimate of the potential impact of higher bonus payments on the number of reenlistments is presented later.

break-even situation over the four-year period; that is, retention costs and replacement costs over the period would be equal. Finally, it is assumed that inducements will be paid to all additional people who reenlist for a second term (after serving for a total of eight years) at the same average rate now being paid to those reenlisting at that point.[20]

On the basis of these assumptions a comparison of the full incremental costs over the 16-year period in which the retention of jobholders would be likely to influence the budget reveals that on balance it is cheaper to retain them than to replace them. Table 5-4 shows that under the assumptions outlined the retention of a typical jobholder beyond the first four years of service would yield savings on the order of $21,000. To the extent that the size of the inducements needed are overstated by the assumptions used in the calculation, savings would be even larger.

Future Prospects

As strong as the implications of this trade-off are for improving the cost-effectiveness of U.S. armed forces, a look toward the future makes the case all the more compelling. The disproportionate growth in costs associated with maintaining a pipeline of young personnel has yet to run its course. Indeed, all indications are that the upward trend will continue since recruitment incentives are bound to grow, and junior personnel may well become eligible for more liberal dependent benefits. It is also possible that the services' needs for specialists will continue to increase, in which case the costs of training are bound to grow further. This all means that replacement costs can be expected to grow relative to retention costs.

Recruitment

Two factors are bound to make recruitment more difficult in the future: (1) the imminent decline in the number of young men in the population as the postwar baby boom runs its course, and (2) the diminishing proportion likely to volunteer as the economy improves.

20. It should be noted that the number of bonuses now paid to those who reenlist beyond the second term are relatively small; in fiscal year 1978, for example, the armed forces made first-installment bonus payments to only about 4,900 military personnel reenlisting for a second or subsequent period, with the total payments amounting to just over $6 million. (Data on bonus payments made available by the Office of the Assistant Secretary of Defense for Manpower, Reserve Affairs, and Logistics.)

Table 5-4. Comparison of Cost Streams Implied by the Replacement or Retention of a Typical Military Enlisted Jobholder (Grade E-4)[a]
Costs in constant fiscal year 1978 dollars

Jobholder's year of service	Probability of jobholder being in work force[b]	Replacement cost[c]	Retention cost				Total
			Longevity[d]	Retirement accrual[e]	Support[f]	Inducement[g]	
5	1.000	9,910	830	850	370	7,860	9,910
6	0.864	8,691	727	746	325	6,893	8,691
7	0.726	7,412	621	636	277	5,878	7,412
8	0.629	6,518	746	1,220	363	4,189	6,518
9	0.537	5,648	646	1,057	314	665	2,682
10	0.475	5,071	591	949	282	588	2,410
11	0.433	4,692	537	878	261	536	2,212
12	0.404	4,443	508	832	247	500	2,087
13	0.380	4,242	485	794	235	...	1,514
14	0.364	4,124	607	1,048	255	...	1,910
15	0.352	4,048	596	1,029	250	...	1,875
16	0.343	4,004	587	1,018	247	...	1,852
17	0.336	3,981	586	1,252	269	...	2,107
18	0.323	3,884	692	1,221	262	...	2,175
19	0.321	3,918	698	1,232	265	...	2,195
20	0.313	3,878	691	1,238	263	...	2,192
Present value of cost stream[h]		71,322	8,319	12,862	3,701	25,439	50,321

Source: Authors' estimates based on assumptions indicated in notes below.

a. Estimates are based on the following assumptions: (1) military pay increases at a rate of 1.5 percent a year in real terms (the same assumption used by the administration to calculate the normal cost of military retirement); (2) promotion of the jobholder in question to E-5 occurs in his sixth year, to E-6 in his eleventh year, to E-7 in his seventeenth year, and to E-8 in his nineteenth year; (3) trained strength and grade structure are held constant; and (4) retirement of the jobholder occurs at the end of his twentieth year of service.

b. Estimates of attrition are based on continuation rates made available by the Office of the Assistant Secretary of Defense for Manpower, Reserve Affairs, and Logistics.

c. Calculated on the assumption that total strength falls (by virtue of reductions in the pipeline) by 1.2 for each jobholder retained. The replacement cost becomes smaller over time, however, to reflect annual attrition among jobholders. To illustrate, the (undiscounted) replacement cost in the jobholder's thirteenth year of service is calculated as follows: $9,910 \times (1.015)^8 \times 0.380 = 4,242$. The term $(1.015)^8$ accounts for the effect of annual real pay increases of 1.5 percent for eight years and 0.380 is the probability that the person is still in the work force. This is an oversimplification of a highly complex and dynamic relationship involving accessions, retention, and the size of the pipeline. It is assumed here that a vacancy at any level can be filled by already available personnel (as is now usually the case) and that by implication each vacancy imposes an equal burden on the pipeline (1.2 new recruits) regardless of the experience level of the worker who left. The application of a single "replacement factor" (that is, 1.2) results in an underestimation of the cost of workers with successively higher levels of experience and of the savings that would be realized by the retention of experienced workers.

d. The incremental cost of longevity pay arises because one billet would now be staffed by a more senior worker and because one less vacancy at a given grade level would necessitate the payment of higher longevity pay to jobholders whose promotions might be deferred at each grade level below.

e. Like longevity pay, the retirement accrual would be higher to the extent that a more senior worker is more likely to retire and also because greater longevity at a given grade implies a higher base pay and thus a larger implicit contribution to military retirement.

f. Includes increases in dependent-related medical and transportation costs resulting from the likelihood that more senior personnel will be married and that they will have more dependents eligible for government benefits.

g. Assumes that the size of bonuses during the first reenlistment period (the fifth through the eighth years of service) could be as large as the difference between replacement cost, on the one hand, and longevity, support, and retirement accrual costs, on the other. The bonus amounts during the second reenlistment period (the ninth through the twelfth years of service) are equivalent to the average bonus paid to those who reenlisted in fiscal year 1978 for the second time. Bonuses are usually paid in equal annual installments for each year of the reenlistment period, an assumption used here. Note, however, that the size of the bonus reflects attrition (or the probability that the jobholder would complete the period of service for which he reenlisted).

h. Calculated by discounting each stream at an interest rate of 2.5 percent in real terms, the same assumption used by the administration to calculate the implicit full funding of federal retirement programs. While the implicit contribution to retirement is highly sensitive to the real interest rate, total retention costs are not, since the bulk of those costs consist of inducements paid early in the 16-year period. To illustrate, at a real interest rate of 2 percent the present value of retirement accrual is 18 percent larger than it is at an interest rate of 2.5 percent, but the present value of total retention costs is only 3 percent greater. On net, the difference between replacement and retention costs at 2 percent interest is $22,017, remarkably close to the difference obtained at 2.5 percent interest.

A few years from now, as the effects of the dwindling birthrates in the 1960s begin to be felt, the number of young men reaching age 18 will decline in an absolute sense. The decline will be sharp; between 1977 and 1985 the number of 18-year-olds will fall by 15 percent and by over 25 percent by 1992. With a smaller source of supply, recruiting will be more difficult; instead of having to attract one of every six males to reach projected recruiting goals, as is now the case, the services eventually will have to attract one of every four. While it should remain possible to meet quantitative requirements, the quality of the manpower recruited will surely suffer.

But difficulties may develop even before the demographic problem is encountered. As the economy recovers, the number of male high school graduates drawn to military service is likely to reach disturbingly low levels. In general the lower the unemployment rate or the less military pay is increased relative to civilian pay, the lower the propensity to volunteer.

Under a wide range of plausible economic assumptions, projected increases in military pay will be insufficient to offset the effects of increased civilian job opportunities. According to one estimate, by 1981 the services will be fortunate to attract 80 percent of their requirement for high school graduates capable of scoring above the thirtieth percentile in standardized tests; by 1985 that figure is likely to decrease to 64 percent.[21] The greater the economic recovery, of course, the greater the shortfall. Thus pressures will mount to increase recruiting and advertising budgets and to provide additional financial incentives; if such increases come to pass the costs associated with personnel turnover will grow even more.

Training

The extent to which the military's needs for highly trained technicians will continue to expand in the future is highly uncertain. Some factors could increase the requirements for skilled personnel, while others could have the opposite effect. Among the former is the introduction of new technologies, some of which are only now on the drawing board. Barring

21. Estimate based on data contained in Congressional Budget Office, *National Service Programs and Their Effects on Military Manpower and Civilian Youth Problems* (GPO, 1978), p. 13. It is worth noting, however, that the supply of experienced workers, that is, those in the prime productive years (25–54), will increase sharply during the period. Thus unless economic recovery is especially vigorous, youth unemployment could conceivably remain high.

major breakthroughs, however, it stretches the imagination to perceive more than modest changes in the skill composition of the armed forces. Despite the popularized image of the automated Buck Rogers–style battlefield of the future, characterized by small numbers of highly trained operators remotely commanding electronic tanks and laser death rays, the composition of U.S. ground combat forces can be expected to change little over the next 25 years, if past experience is any guide. Although major advances are expected in precision-guided munitions and perhaps in improved battlefield mobility, the demise of traditional ground formations and their heavy dependence on the combat infantryman seems unlikely.

Although the issue of the future role of the Navy is far from settled, the composition of the fleet in the year 2000 is fairly well determined, given the long lead time associated with shipbuilding programs and the long life expectancies of these expensive naval systems. The Navy's need for skilled personnel is certain to increase in absolute terms if only because of the projected increase in the number of naval vessels. Moreover, the roster of skills is likely to become even more heavily dominated by specialists and technicians since the new ships that will enter the fleet over the next two decades are bound to have more sophisticated electronic systems and more complex propulsion plants than are installed in the older ships being replaced. The extent of the change in the Navy's skill mix is hard to predict, but it could be quite sizable, particularly if the Navy relies to a greater extent on nuclear propulsion.

The Air Force's roster of skills, already dominated by technicians, is unlikely to experience more than modest changes over the next two decades. Aircraft and missile systems now in the research and development stage by and large represent improvements in the state of the art rather than revolutionary change. For example, as matters stand, wide-bodied jets armed with cruise missiles are likely to constitute the manned portion of the strategic triad at the turn of the century. At that time the generation of fighter aircraft to follow the F-15/F-16 will probably be operational; there is nothing to indicate changes in design, deployment, or organization of tactical air forces sufficient to warrant changes in the manpower skill mix. One development that could lead to major changes for the Air Force manpower mix would be an extensive commitment to the military's role in space. But given the level of effort now being expended in that direction, the long lead times involved, and the absence of a discernible threat, this possibility must be discounted.

Working against further increases in technical skill requirements is the prospect that technological developments will reduce the maintenance work load. This speculation centers on the premise that advances in weapon system design should reduce the need for highly skilled electronic technicians capable of dismantling and repairing sophisticated equipment and instead make possible the maximum use of modular components that can be removed, replaced, and returned for repair to civilian-manned depots.

In sum, projecting military occupational requirements is an uncertain proposition subject to a wide variety of unpredictable influences. It seems safe to conclude, however, that the military's requirements for trained specialists will continue to increase, as will training costs, though probably at a slower rate.

Dependent-Related Costs

Until recently, when reassigned from one location to another, junior enlisted personnel (those in grade E-4 and below with less than two years of service) were not entitled to have their dependents accompany them at government expense. Many of these people nevertheless moved their families and belongings at their own expense, which gave rise to dissatisfaction among those involved. Accordingly, in 1978 the administration requested $103 million to extend dependent travel and transportation entitlements to everyone transferred to or from an overseas location regardless of grade and years of service.[22] Subsequently Congress approved about $95 million for this purpose.[23] Furthermore, the President's Commission on Military Compensation has recommended extending entitlement even further to cover transfers within the United States, and this would cost an estimated additional $113 million annually (in fiscal 1979 dollars).[24]

---

22. *Department of Defense Authorization for Appropriations for Fiscal Year 1979,* Hearings before the Senate Committee on Armed Services, 95 Cong 2 sess. (GPO, 1978), pt. 3: *Manpower and Personnel,* p. 2082.

23. See *Department of Defense Appropriations Bill, 1979,* H. Rept. 95-1398, 95 Cong. 2 sess. (GPO, 1978), pp. 19–20; and *Congressional Record,* daily edition, October 12, 1978, pt. II, p. H12572. Further proposals to improve the status of junior personnel in the volunteer force can be expected, thus continuing the upward pressure on pipeline costs.

24. *Report of the President's Commission on Military Compensation* (GPO, 1978), pp. 156–57.

Potential for Change

On the basis of the discussion above, the widely held belief that a more experienced armed force can be shaped only at the expense of increasing the size of the defense budget can be disputed. Indeed, the foregoing analysis suggests that as a result of substantial increases in the cost of the personnel pipeline, this nation may not be getting the maximum payoff for its investment in military manpower. Moreover, in view of the cost trends it is clear that the advantages of shaping a more experienced military force will become even greater in the future. Steps to shape such a force, then, should be taken now.

Because the experience level of the military forces is inextricably intertwined with other facets of the military personnel management system, the extent to which appropriate changes can be made in worker retention patterns without concurrent changes in pay and promotion policies is sharply curtailed. This is not to say, however, that enhancement of the experience mix is not possible within the present policy framework. In fact, in this section the possibilities for enriching the experience composition of the armed forces in the short run are explored. A discussion of more far-reaching modifications in the experience mix, calling for fundamental changes in the way the military manages its personnel and for substantial changes in legislation, is deferred until the next chapter.

Fewer Losses, More Reenlistments

To appreciate the potential for improvement, it is useful to examine the nature and extent of job vacancies as they now occur. Table 5-5 shows the distribution of losses of trained enlisted personnel by major occupational category in fiscal year 1977, the most recent year for which detailed data are available. All in all, about 317,000, or 21 percent, of all trained enlisted personnel left the services in that year; over half of these were technicians and craftsmen, almost one-third were personnel serving in the combat arms or in service and supply jobs, and the remainder were in clerical positions. As can be seen, loss rates, high as they appear in absolute terms, show little variation when adjusted by occupational area; technical workers, for example, leave the military at about the same rate as clerical personnel do, and this is inconsistent with the differences in training investments embodied in these individuals.

Table 5-5. Losses of Trained Enlisted Personnel, by Major Occupational Category, Fiscal Year 1977

Major occupational category[a]	Enlisted personnel losses	
	Number	Percent
Technical workers	**84,013**	**20**
Electronic equipment repairmen	28,860	
Communications and intelligence specialists	30,866	
Medical and dental specialists	16,446	
Other technical and allied specialists	7,841	
Clerical workers[b]	**50,133**	**19**
Craftsmen	**87,529**	**21**
Electrical/mechanical equipment repairmen	70,634	
All other craftsmen	16,895	
Other	**95,505**	**23**
Infantry, gun crews, and seamanship specialists	59,495	
Service and supply handlers	36,010	
All categories	**317,180**	**21**

Source: Unpublished data provided by the Office of the Assistant Secretary of Defense for Manpower, Reserve Affairs, and Logistics.

a. Categories are based on the Department of Defense occupational classification system discussed in chapter 3.

b. The "functional support and administration" category.

To redress these imbalances fully would call for fundamental changes in the military personnel management system, and many would view them as long-term propositions. Such changes as would probably be warranted for a more rational retention pattern in the long run merit careful study, and some are outlined in the next chapter. In the short term, barring major modifications in the structure of military compensation and length-of-service policies, the extent to which improvements in retention can be made is limited. Since the number of annual retirements is not controlled, for all practical purposes the potential supply of experienced personnel that the armed forces can tap exists largely in the first-term enlisted population—in those people who are completing their initial enlistment obligation (generally after four years) and who are eligible to reenlist. In the short run, then, improving retention where experience counts the most would require a concentrated effort to increase the number of first-term reenlistments among trained technicians and craftsmen.

But how much of an increase in the first-term reenlistment rate is it reasonable to expect at the level of inducements earmarked in the break-even calculation in table 5-4? According to Pentagon estimates of the relationship between reenlistment rates and financial inducements, an improvement of about 25 percent in the first-term reenlistment rate could be achieved. This increase would yield about 14,000 reenlistments over the number attained in fiscal year 1978.[25] For illustration, the costs and benefits associated with the retention of an additional 14,000 trained enlisted personnel are examined below.

Implications for the Budget

Table 5-6 compares the costs that could be incurred at the higher level of retention with the costs that would result from replacement. Starting with 14,000 as the number of additional reenlistees in their fifth year of service, the table shows the number expected to remain in the military in subsequent years, according to current attrition estimates. As before, it is assumed here that the number of trained persons and the grade distribution of the jobs to which they are assigned is held fixed, while the size of the pipeline is reduced so that for every 100 jobholders retained, 120 replacements would not have to be recruited, processed, and trained. Under this assumption an increase in the number of reenlistments by 14,000 means that 14,000 jobs normally staffed by workers with less than five years of service would now be staffed by personnel in their fifth year (a necessity, if reenlistment is possible only at the completion of four years of service). Naturally, this also means that if those retained are to remain in their jobs, say at the E-4 grade level, some less experienced workers who would otherwise have been promoted (perhaps prematurely) from the E-3 to the E-4 grade level to fill such vacancies, would now remain in their E-3 jobs. The conditions for granting promotions to qualified persons would be met to the extent that vacancies would occur, as is now the case. It is not reasonable to assume that promotion opportunities now

25. Derived from data presented in Department of Defense Instruction 1304.22, Enclosure 4, p. 6. The reenlistment improvement factors incorporated in the instruction were based on the earlier work of John H. Enns, *Reenlistment Bonuses and First-Term Retention,* prepared for the Defense Advanced Research Projects Agency, ARPA 189-1, R-1935 (Rand Corporation, 1977). These factors indicate that a fourfold increase in the total dollar amount of first-term bonus payments would yield a 25 percent increase in the fiscal year 1978 first-term reenlistment rate (or 14,000 reenlistees). This aggregate estimate is probably conservative since the calculation is based on the assumption that the increased reenlistments would occur proportionally across all occupations. In fact, if the additional bonus payments were concentrated in high-skill categories, which now experience relatively lower retention rates, it is possible that more than 14,000 additional reenlistments could be induced.

Table 5-6. Comparison of Cost Streams Implied by a 25 Percent Increase in the First-Term Reenlistment Rate among Military Enlisted Jobholders (Grade E-4)[a]

Year of service of reenlistment cohort	Number of reenlistees remaining in the work force	Replacement cost		Retention cost	
		Per capita[b] (dollars)	Total (millions of dollars)	Per capita[b] (dollars)	Total (millions of dollars)
5	14,000	9,910	139	9,910	139
6	12,096	10,059	122	10,059	122
7	10,164	10,210	104	10,210	104
8	8,806	10,363	91	10,363	91
9	7,518	10,518	79	4,994	38
10	6,650	10,676	71	5,074	34
11	6,062	10,836	66	5,109	31
12	5,656	10,999	62	5,166	29
13	5,320	11,164	59	3,984	21
14	5,096	11,331	58	5,247	27
15	4,928	11,501	57	5,327	26
16	4,802	11,673	56	5,399	26
17	4,704	11,849	56	6,271	29
18	4,522	12,026	54	6,734	30
19	4,494	12,207	55	6,838	31
20	4,382	12,390	54	7,003	31
Present value of cost stream			999		705

Source: Authors' estimates derived from data presented in table 5-4.

a. Costs are in constant fiscal year 1978 dollars.

b. Per capita costs for the sixth through twentieth year derived by same method employed to calculate costs for fifth year, as shown in table 5-3.

available to enlisted workers have no relation to merit or that the armed forces can promise promotions when they cannot (and to the extent that they do not) promise or control vacancies. Nevertheless, the cost estimates developed here include higher longevity payments, thus partially offsetting the financial cost to the individual of a deferred promotion.

While the staffing changes considered in this illustration are quite modest, involving only about 14,000 of some 1.5 million jobs, they nevertheless do affect the experience composition of the enlisted force and hence the budget needed to sustain it for as long as these additional reenlistees remain in the force. Manning 14,000 jobs with workers somewhat more experienced for their grade (E-4) implies that those serving in positions at grades below the E-4 level are also more experienced. As a result, the longevity component of the compensation costs, dependent-related support costs, and the costs of retirement of the more experienced force considered here would increase over and above their present levels. Table 5-6 shows the incremental cost of retention (that is, additional longevity, support, and retirement-related costs) that should be added to the current cost of filling the positions under consideration in this illustration. On the other hand, while the number of jobholders remains the same, the number of job vacancies has been reduced; the corresponding replacement costs have not been incurred and will not be incurred for as long as any of the additional 14,000 reenlistees remain in the enlisted force.

As can be seen, retention costs and replacement costs are equal for the first four years, allowing for an incremental bonus cost sufficient to attract the initial 14,000 additional reenlistments and to enable the armed forces to continue paying the annual bonus installments to all personnel remaining in the service for the full four-year term. Beyond that period, however, monetary savings could be expected to mount as the costs of replacement outran the costs of retention. Over the full sixteen-year period, costs associated with the retention of the 14,000 trained personnel in the illustration would amount to about 70 percent of the costs that would have to be incurred if, everything else being equal, the additional reenlistments had not been attracted. To the extent that improvements in the first-term reenlistment rate could be maintained year after year, financial savings—estimated to be nearly $300 million in the illustration above—could be expected to grow. More important than the monetary savings, however, is that enrichment of the experience mix would enhance U.S. military effectiveness.

Implications for Personnel Quality

So far it has been emphasized that increases in the rate of retention will enable the armed forces to improve the utilization of experienced personnel, thereby reducing reliance on accessions inflows. It should be noted, however, that other though less direct benefits can be reaped by the military as accessions requirements are reduced.

To the extent that the armed forces could pursue lower quantitative goals, they would be apt to simultaneously set higher qualitative enlistment standards and criteria. The sense of the military community regarding recruit quality was expressed by a senior defense official: "We emphasize male high school diploma graduate recruiting to gain the potential savings in training and reduced personnel turbulence that results from lower attrition. . . . we will accept fewer non-[high school] graduates as total accessions drop next year."[26] Thus insofar that recruit quality could improve, a costless increase in future retention rates could be secured: a fall in first-term attrition—a reasonable expectation—would serve to enlarge the pool of potential reenlistees and hence to increase the number of reenlistments in the short run. Naturally such a development would further promote manpower utilization in the military and thus enhance force effectiveness over the long run.

CONSIDERATION has been given to short-term changes that could allow the enlisted force to mature, to acquire more skill and expertise, and thus to perform more effectively. The purpose of this chapter has not been to prescribe quantitative solutions but rather to discuss and demonstrate possibilities. The modest increase in the reenlistment rate illustrated here under quite conservative assumptions could most likely be sustained in the future, yielding larger real savings over time. Or it may be that the potential for change in the short run is even greater than this discussion has suggested. For example, seeking to improve retention by limiting the number of annual retirements (especially at grades above the E-7 level) would reduce the retention cost even further; persons whose retirement is postponed need not receive additional financial inducements, and the payment of their military pensions would be deferred. And it may be that a more rational and less cumbersome structure of military compensation would make retention pay off even more. To the extent that both of these institutional variables (the retirement system in particular and the level and structure of military compensation in general) are used so as to emphasize youthfulness and vigor, their function may no longer be appropriate.

26. White statement in *Department of Defense Appropriations for 1979,* Hearings, pt. 3, pp. 12–13.

CHAPTER SIX

REFORMS FOR THE LONG TERM

WHILE ENHANCEMENT of the experience mix of the armed forces can begin within the existing policy framework, more fundamental reforms would have to be undertaken before the full potential of military manpower could be utilized. As pointed out in the previous chapter, the potential for change in personnel retention is now constrained in two ways.

First, under current policies the maximum length of military service of enlisted personnel does not as a rule exceed 20 years; under the present rules many military personnel find it more advantageous to retire and receive a pension than to serve beyond 20 years and receive their regular pay. This need not be so. Indeed, the evidence presented earlier in this study indicates that improved utilization of military personnel in the long run calls for longer terms of service, consistent with lower turnover among enlisted jobholders. Removing the disincentives to longevity in the armed forces can improve the outlook. To this end, reform of the military retirement system would be necessary.

Second, to the extent that the skill composition of the military work force is implicit in the grade composition, improvements in the skill mix of enlisted personnel should ultimately produce changes in the grade structure, thereby altering both the distribution of military earnings and promotion opportunities. Consequently modifications in the personnel management system would be needed. In this chapter, then, the more fundamental reforms necessary for improved manpower utilization in the military are briefly outlined.

Military Retirement Reform

The military retirement system is unique in both purpose and cost. Its purpose has been the maintenance of a youthful and vigorous military force characterized by high turnover rates, and its pensions are considerably more generous than civilian annuities, especially those offered by private employers. Military pension costs were two-fifths as large as the total payroll for the active forces in fiscal year 1979.

The present retirement system may have been appropriate in earlier times, but evidence presented in this study suggests that the purpose the system was originally designed to serve may no longer be relevant. Consequently the costs associated with the present system are becoming exceedingly difficult to justify.

Assumptions and Purposes

Voluntary retirement after only twenty years of service produces large annual outflows of productive military personnel from the armed forces and into civilian employment. Military retirees as a rule can still be gainfully employed; indeed, several studies indicate that almost all of them pursue civilian careers.[1] This is not surprising. By one estimate about 75 percent of enlisted personnel who retire do so after 20 or 21 years of service and the typical new enlisted retiree is only 39 years old.[2]

The validity of the main assumption on which the present retirement system is based was challenged in chapter 3:[3] youthfulness and vigor—still important in some military jobs—should now be de-emphasized as criteria for manning the modern military. It follows that to the extent the military retirement system was once designed to promote a youthful force, its main feature—the 20-year-service minimum—is now obsolete and counterproductive.[4]

Indeed, similar conclusions have been drawn in at least two major studies on military manpower and compensation issues, one of which

1. See, for example, Alan E. Fechter and Bette S. Mahoney, "The Economics of Military Retirement," Research Paper P-414 (Institute for Defense Analyses, July 1967).

2. Congressional Budget Office, *The Military Retirement System: Options for Change*, Budget Issue Paper for Fiscal Year 1979 (Government Printing Office, 1978), p. 6.

3. It has been challenged elsewhere, as well. See, for example, Defense Manpower Commission, *Defense Manpower: The Keystone of National Security*, Report to the President and the Congress, April 1976 (GPO, 1976), especially chap. 8.

4. Over three decades ago during hearings in 1945 before the Senate Committee on Naval Affairs, Senator Charles Andrews expressed reservations about the retirement law allowing military personnel to retire "at the very pinnacle of usefulness. At 45 men are supposed to be at their best mentally, although not physically always, but they are still pretty good physically if they have taken care of themselves." (Quoted in CBO, *The Military Retirement System*, p. 11.)

focuses almost exclusively on military retirement systems.[5] And most of the recommendations for reform point to the logical need for increasing the minimum length of service, restructuring the size of the pensions, and improving equity by distributing retirement benefits to more people. The most recent comprehensive study of the retirement issue prepared by the President's Commission on Military Compensation calls for vested retirement benefits after the tenth year of service and deferred payment of annuities depending on the number of years of service.[6]

Nature of Reform

Yet it would appear that reform should involve more than that. It is significant that the commission's plan includes provisions specifically designed to influence retention behavior.[7] But *should* the retirement system be used as a variable in promoting retention among military personnel?

To answer this question, it is important to consider the alternatives. The present retirement system is the product of the paternalistic system of an earlier era when cash payments constituted only a small part of military remuneration; the remainder was in the form of fringe benefits, of which retirement was the most important. Naturally the shaping of a career force in the past depended heavily on retirement benefits. But times have changed; by most accounts military pay is now on a par with federal

5. Defense Manpower Commission, *Defense Manpower* and *Report of the President's Commission on Military Compensation* (GPO, 1978).

6. The President's Commission on Military Compensation established by President Carter in 1977 recommended a plan for deferred payment of annuities; the size of the annuity would vary with the number of years of service, reaching a maximum of 90 percent of base income. Under this plan, military personnel would become eligible for a retirement annuity after completing the tenth year of service. A deferred compensation of government-paid trust fund would be established for each member with at least five years of service. After the tenth year members would have the option to withdraw up to 50 percent of the credits in a lump sum or in installments and to return to civilian life. The portion that is not withdrawn would accumulate interest and could be used to supplement the retirement annuity. In addition the plan calls for integrating the military retirement system with the social security system; at present, military retirees receive the benefits of both. For a detailed discussion of the proposed plan see *Report of the President's Commission on Military Compensation*.

7. The commission suggested that allowing members to withdraw up to 50 percent of the value of government-paid credits after 10 years of service and to return to civilian life, accumulating interest on the portion not withdrawn, would reduce retention rates among personnel in the middle grades and would improve retention among junior personnel and among people in top grades.

civilian pay. Moreover, military pay now accounts for a much larger proportion of total military compensation than was the case in the past, especially since the elimination of conscription. Military pay—not pension benefits as currently used—provides the armed services with a sufficient number of volunteers. Similarly, military pay and not pension benefits should be the primary means to promote retention and enrich the experience mix of the military labor force.

Reform of the military retirement system is still a long-term proposition. Yet viewed in the perspective outlined above, such a reform should not prove difficult to implement. Since military pay is now in line with federal civilian pay, it would be reasonable to allow military personnel to retire in much the same way their federal civilian counterparts do, leaving the achievement of personnel retention goals as a function to be performed mainly by military pay rates and the distribution of military earnings.[8]

Reforms in the Grade Structure

To be implemented successfully, military retirement reform should be accompanied by changes in the military personnel management system, now unduly constrained by the grade structure of enlisted jobs. To understand the nature of this constraint, it is useful to examine the present relationship between the grade structure of military jobs and the skill composition of the workers who fill them.

Table 6-1 shows the distribution of enlisted military personnel by grade and occupational category. Pay grades are arrayed in three skill groups: the lower grades E-1 through E-3 may be thought of as corresponding to the apprenticeship level; grades E-4 to E-7, the journeyman

8. Variants of such a plan have been examined elsewhere. For example, in a study by the Congressional Budget Office plans calling for annuities at age 55, combined with or without a contribution, have been considered. According to the study: "A judgment that the military could accomplish its role with a substantially older force suggests an option like the annuity-at-55 option, with its higher risk but accompanying higher potential for savings." (CBO, *The Military Retirement System*, p. 66.) Naturally, the risk arises if implementation of such a plan is not preceded by a restructuring of military compensation. (An employee contribution would serve to reduce pay, everything else being equal. In addition vested retirement benefits might induce losses among personnel in the middle grades, everything else being equal.) Restructuring pay so as to strengthen retention incentives is a quid pro quo for military retirement reform.

Table 6-1. Distribution of Enlisted Personnel by Grade and Occupational Category, 1977
Percent

	Grade		
*Occupational category*ᵃ	*E-1 to E-3*	*E-4 to E-7*	*E-8 to E-9*
Technical workers			
Electronic equipment repairmen	17	79	4
Communications and intelligence specialists	29	68	3
Medical and dental specialists	29	69	2
Other technical and allied specialists	25	72	3
Clerical workers			
Administrative specialists and clerks	21	74	5
Craftsmen			
Electrical/mechanical equipment repairmen	29	68	2
All other craftsmen	31	67	2
Other			
Infantry, gun crews, and seamanship specialists	38	60	3
Service and supply handlers	35	64	2

Source: Unpublished data provided by Office of Assistant Secretary of Defense for Manpower, Reserve Affairs, and Logistics. Percentages are rounded.
a. Based on the Department of Defense occupational classification system discussed in chapter 3.

level; and grades E-8 and E-9, the highest skill level (proficiency in a wide range of jobs and supervisory responsibilities).

While grade distributions differ somewhat by occupation, the differences are not nearly as great as those that would be expected in view of the relative value of experience. For example, the proportion of journeymen is about the same in the craft jobs as in the service and supply jobs; and the number of personnel in the highest grades is almost fixed at between 2 and 3 percent in all occupational areas with the exception of the clerical jobs. Indeed, the grade structure of clerical jobs deserves closer examination; in these jobs the proportion of workers in grades E-4 and above is second only to the proportion of journeymen in electronic repair. This would appear to imply that the armed forces place greater emphasis on expertise in the clerical jobs than expertise in, say, the craftsmen jobs. In fact, the rationale underlying the whole grade distribution is far from clear. As table 6-2 shows, it is difficult to distinguish occupational areas from one another on the basis of mean grade, which varies from 4.0 for infantry, gun crews, and seamanship specialists to 4.8 for clerical and electronic equipment repairmen. This similarity in mean grades would be inconsequential in the absence of differences in market value of the different skills military personnel possessed. Such differences, however, are sure to exist. It is well known that significant occupational wage differentials distinguish electricians from cooks and from clerks in the civilian sector. Among male full-time, full-year workers in civilian employment, professional and technical workers earn an average of about 55 percent more than unskilled workers.[9] Faced with this situation, the armed forces should be in a position to compete effectively for personnel, not just at the entry level, but what is perhaps more important, at the higher levels as well. Yet the distribution of military grades—and of earnings determined thereby does not adequately differentiate personnel by occupational area, thus underscoring the need for change.[10]

This situation may have contributed to the formation of the undesirable retention rate patterns discussed in chapter 5. Because the average compensation is about the same regardless of occupational area, the armed forces are essentially offering equal pay to workers performing unequal jobs (unequal in the sense of "different"), thus paying some workers more than they have to and other workers less than they ought to.

The services have attempted to correct for the effect of pay imbalances, mainly by offering bonuses to prospective reenlistees. Apart from the uncertainties involved in projecting future manning requirements and hence in determining the appropriate size of the bonuses at a given time, the effectiveness of bonuses may be questioned on at least two grounds. First, whether the bonus is paid in a lump sum or in installments it may fail to be adequately perceived as a part of pay. Second, and more important, since the offer of a bonus does not automatically imply a promotion, the use of bonuses may still leave the underlying grade structure unaffected.

To remedy this problem, reform of the grade structure of military jobs is warranted. As one alternative, military pay rates could be made to vary explicitly by occupational area. This would require a variety of pay tables

9. U.S. Bureau of the Census, *Census of Population, 1970,* Subject Reports: *Occupational Characteristics,* Final Report PC(2)-7A (GPO, 1973), table 1, pp. 1–11.

10. Military "earnings" are in the form of regular military compensation, defined as the sum of basic pay, basic allowance for quarters, basic allowance for subsistence, and the tax advantage that accrues because quarters and subsistence allowances are not taxed. Basic pay varies by grade; basic allowance for quarters (when offered in cash) varies by grade and number of dependents; basic allowance for subsistence is offered at fixed per diem rates. In addition to regular military compensation, enlisted members may, if qualified, receive additional kinds of pay (incentive, proficiency, and so on), bonuses (enlistment and reenlistment), and allowances; these compensation components also vary by pay grade. For a detailed discussion of the military pay system see Martin Binkin, *The Military Pay Muddle* (Brookings Institution, 1975).

Table 6-2. Average Grade and Average Time in Service for All Enlisted Personnel, by Occupational Category, 1977

Occupational category[a]	Average grade	Average years in service
Infantry, gun crews, and seamanship specialists	4.0	4.7
Electronic equipment repairmen	4.8	7.3
Communications and intelligence specialists	4.4	6.2
Medical and dental specialists	4.4	6.0
Other technical and allied specialists	4.6	7.1
Administrative specialists and clerks	4.8	8.0
Electrical/mechanical repairmen	4.3	6.0
Craftsmen	4.4	6.6
Service and supply handlers	4.2	6.1

Source: Unpublished data provided by the Office of the Assistant Secretary of Defense for Manpower, Reserve Affairs, and Logistics.

a. Based on Department of Defense occupational classification system discussed in chapter 3.

appropriate for the current grade structure.[11] Another alternative—less complicated but also less apt to be accepted by military traditionalists— that could accomplish the same purpose would involve grade restructuring: occupations would be clearly distinguished from one another by the number of pay grades for which they are defined; not all jobs would be defined at all grade levels. Thus, for example, while a worker in electronics could advance to the E-9 grade level over the course of his career, a person in service and supply would reach only, say, the E-5 grade level. For the service and supply worker, further advancement would require occupational mobility, as is the case with most civilian employees. This could easily be accomplished in the military (for qualified workers and subject to the availability of positions) through successful completion of the appropriate training curriculum.

Grade restructuring of military jobs would alter the distribution of advancement opportunities in the armed forces; at present the distribution of advancement opportunities is neither efficient nor equitable. Table 6-2 shows the average time in service and average grade by occupational area, and in a sense these figures show the average length of time involved in the attainment of the average grade.[12] Thus, for example, after six years of

11. This concept is not without precedent. For British volunteers basic pay depends on rank and length of service but also on length of commitment and, significantly, on the enlisted person's "trade group," or occupational area. For a description of the British system see Stewart W. Kemp, "British Experience with an All-Volunteer Armed Force," *Studies Prepared for the President's Commission on an All-Volunteer Armed Force,* November 1970 [GPO, 1971], vol. 2, pp. III-4-12– III-4-16.

12. It is assumed, in other words, that differential promotion opportunities may in effect produce wage differentials.

service the typical service and supply worker has attained the E-4 grade; but so has the typical jobholder in communications and intelligence and in electrical/mechanical repair. This tradition, too, has its roots in an earlier era when military personnel were much more homogeneous in terms of the skills they possessed and the tasks they performed, but today the armed forces are characterized by a diversified labor force. Moreover, "equality" in military pay and promotion opportunities was feasible— though not necessarily justifiable—when the military services made use of conscripted manpower and pay was equally low for all, but today the armed forces are facing the challenge of competing for workers. Under the circumstances, and in a (well-understood) spirit of egalitarianism, advancement opportunities in the military should be realigned and made consistent with occupational requirements, thereby improving manpower utilization and hence the effectiveness of the armed forces.

THE MEASURES proposed above—reforming the armed forces' retirement system and revamping the military's grade structure—would create a framework within which a balance between youth and experience more appropriate to the needs of the emerging military establishment could be struck.

Realistically, these reforms cannot be accomplished overnight. Although the retirement system has been subjected to close scrutiny in recent years, resulting proposals, though well-intentioned, have missed the mark. This does not necessarily mean a return to the drawing board, but it suggests that larger issues should be settled first. What is the appropriate distribution of skills in the armed forces and hence of ages and grades? What is the level and structure of compensation that will enable the armed forces to achieve and maintain this skill composition? This study is but a first step in pursuing answers to these questions. Much remains to be done; research and planning should begin at once.

It is important, however, that these longer-term questions not stand in the way of immediately exploiting the opportunities for increasing the effectiveness of U.S. military forces that are available within the current policy framework. In this respect the Pentagon should take steps to improve retention among certain experienced personnel, thereby reducing the demands for new volunteers and for the resources now devoted to maintaining a relatively large pool of nonproductive employees. These steps not only would allow the nation to field more effective armed forces but could save money as well.